Adventure Games

Zondervan/Youth Specialties Books

Adventure Games

Amazing Tension Getters

Called to Care

The Complete Student
Missions Handbook

Creative Socials and Special Events

Divorce Recovery for Teenagers

Feeding Your Forgotten Soul
(Spiritual Growth for Youth Workers)

Get 'Em Talking

Good Clean Fun

Good Clean Fun, Volume 2

Great Games for 4th–6th Graders
(Get 'Em Growing)

Great Ideas for Small Youth Groups

Greatest Skits on Earth

Greatest Skits on Earth, Volume 2

Growing Up in America

High School Ministry

High School TalkSheets

Holiday Ideas for Youth Groups
(Revised Edition)

Hot Talks

Ideas for Social Action

Intensive Care:
Helping Teenagers in Crisis

Junior High Ministry

Junior High TalkSheets

The Ministry of Nurture

On-Site: 40 On-Location Programs
for Youth Groups

Option Plays

Organizing Your Youth Ministry

Play It! Great Games for Groups

Teaching the Bible Creatively

Teaching the Truth about Sex

Tension Getters

Tension Getters II

Unsung Heroes: How to Recruit
and Train Volunteer Youth Workers

Up Close and Personal: How to Build
Community in Your Youth Group

Youth Specialties Clip Art Book

Youth Specialties Clip Art Book,
Volume 2

Adventure Games
Creative Outdoor Activities for Your Youth Group

Jeff Hopper
Steve Torrey
Rod Yonkers

Zondervan Publishing House
Grand Rapids, Michigan

Disclaimer

This book (like life) contains games that, in an unfortunate combination of circumstances, could result in emotional or physical harm. You'll need to evaluate each game on its own merit for your group, for each game's potential risk, for safety precautions that must be taken, advance preparation that must be made, and possible results before you use a game. Youth Specialties, Inc., is not responsible—nor has it any control over—the use or misuse of any of the games published in this book.

Adventure Games

Copyright © 1990 by Youth Specialties, Inc.

Youth Specialties Books, 1224 Greenfield Drive, El Cajon, California 92021,
are published by Zondervan Publishing House,
Grand Rapids, Michigan 49530

Library of Congress Cataloging-in-Publication Data

Hopper, Jeff, 1963–
Adventure games / Jeff Hopper, Steve "Buck" Torrey, Rod "Bernie" Yonkers
p.   cm.
ISBN 0-310-52871-2
1. Adventure games.   2. Group games.   I. Torrey, Steve, 1956–.   II. Yonkers, Rod, 1954–.   III. Title.
GV1203.H572   1990
793.93'2--dc20   90-34185
                                                                                                          CIP

All Scripture quotations, unless otherwise noted, are taken from the *Holy Bible: New International Version* (North American Edition). Copyright © 1973, 1978, 1984 by the International Bible Society. Used by permission of Zondervan Bible Publishers.

Edited by Leslie Emmons
Cover design by Mark Rayburn
Illustrated by Dan Pegoda
Author photograph by Roger Monroe
Book design by JamisonBell Advertising and Design
Printed in the United States of America

94 95 96 97 98 99 / CH / 10 9 8 7 6 5 4 3

To:
Jim and Manya Slevcove
and Yosemite Sierra Summer Camp
"Home of the World's Greatest Campers"

All of life may not be a great adventure,
but all adventure may be brought to life.

Adventure Games

Preface

As children, we kept in good physical shape because we were always playing in the yard, riding bikes, jumping rope, swimming, or climbing trees. And we stayed in good mental shape because we played in imagination.

We became the characters in our forts, the dolls in our doll houses, the soldiers in our battlefields, the sports heroes in our stadiums. We lived all that we imagined because we vicariously placed ourselves in the middle of the situations our minds had created. We could determine the endings of our games, which were really just the beginnings to new adventures. We could live again if we wanted. We could go back to the second out in the bottom of the ninth inning—this time with the bases loaded when we came to bat.

Adventure games give us the unique opportunity to renew the imagination of our childhoods. They provide exercise for our bodies and our minds. But beyond providing mental and physical exercise, adventure games take us out of our current world, away from the day's pressures and problems. Adventure games demand that we enter another world in which we create the events that happen. We imagine and we dream in ways that we forgot were possible.

This book is more than a compilation of fun games to play with a group. In many ways, it is a cry for all of us to use our imaginations again, tapping the creativity God has given us to use.

These games were designed and enhanced at Yosemite Sierra Summer Camp, a program for 4th through 12th graders. Yet, we have found these games to be adaptable to various environments, including parks, campuses, and empty fields. The games are described in each chapter specifically enough to understand the goals, rules, and requirements, but generally enough for you to be changed for your group and your area. The outlines are included to help you select a game or to use as a reference in your preparation.

We have three hopes for you. First, we hope that you will become excited about playing adventure games and that you will stretch your imagination in new and different directions. Second, we hope that you will be a stimulus to others by setting up adventures for them to play and live. Third, we hope that you will create your own adventure games based on your renewed imagination and the thrill you see in others playing adventure games.

How to Use the Outlines in *Adventure Games*

At the very end of each chapter of this book you will find in outline form the instructions that we have given you for playing the games in this book. They are included as an aid in preparing these games and can serve several useful purposes.

Supply lists. These lists include all items necessary to play the specified games, but without the detailed instructions that accompany them in the chapter. After reading the chapter, you may want to use the list in the outline as a quick reference and checklist.

Choosing games. When you need to find a game that will fit a certain theme, playing site, or playing time, the outlines are a speedier way to do so.

Telling the story. If you decide that you would like to tell the story without using the scripts included in the various chapters, make a copy of the needed outline. By referring to the condensed version of the rules as you tell your story, you can be sure that you haven't missed anything important.

We hope that you will use these outlines and that they will help you run your games easily and effectively.

Acknowledgments

These games were developed at Yosemite Sierra Summer Camp, our inspiration for many summers. Our first and warmest expression of gratitude goes to our camp director, Jim "Kimo" Slevcove, who gave us the freedom to try these new games and who is of constant encouragement to us.

Thanks are due to those who helped develop some of the early games: Dave Hoehl, Bill Barnes, Roy Cress, and "Tiger" England. Thanks also to some of the energetic players who helped us refine these games: Josh and Kabe Grant, Joe Slevcove, Jethro, Mishko, Badger, Zack, Mav, and the notorious Judd Halenza.

There were individuals who brought creativity and an extra bit of fun to the games we will always remember: Jeff Brown, Spanky, Jeff Olson, Brent Melville, Brad Thompson, and Mike Corboy, as well as the members of YSLO and the peacemaking food service staff.

We'd also like to give special thanks to those who were there to greet us when we came back to reality, Ron and Margie Grant, J.P. and Pam Phillips, and to Laura and Pam, who always had the most fun incamps.

Thanks to Robin Agee, Wayne Rice, and Gary Richardson who reviewed the first draft of the book, and to Noel Becchetti, who pushed it into reality.

CHAPTER ONE

The Strength of
Adventure

I T APPEARED OUT OF NOWHERE on the far side of the meadow, away from our teepees. The kids were already asleep, but we were just settling down for the night. We then saw it in the darkness—the flash of a siren-like red light. Next we heard an eerie, electronic sound pulsating through the wilderness.

We weren't at all prepared for what happened next. There in the darkness, lit only by the glow of the red light, we saw a shiny, silver creature walk a few steps and disappear into the night.

"Look, you guys! It's a UFO!" we shouted, shaking the kids awake with trembling voices. But the kids didn't react. Only a few woke up and even they weren't thrilled about opening their eyes at midnight. So we yelled at them, kicked them, rolled them, jostled them, and bothered them thoroughly. But still there was no real reaction.

Looking back now, it seems foolish to have been disappointed that the kids did not share our excitement. How did we expect them to react to a box of aluminum foil anyway? Could we really expect to create an authentic space fantasy from a sheet of shiny alloy?

That's right—the UFO was our invention. After a day-long rainstorm we were tired of being cooped up and needed some excitement. So when we unearthed a box of foil, we wanted to believe that we could create anything from it, even a flying saucer complete with an alien or two. We grabbed a discount store light from the loft of a cabin, created some feedback on a portable speaker system, lit a highway flare, and mummified one of our leaders in a shroud of foil. The rest of us then went to bed and pretended to sleep, waiting for the adventure to begin.

A half hour later we had a couple of excited yet frightened kids on our hands and we were still waiting for a response from the rest of the group. Although we had created the event of the year, only two kids got up to see it. It seemed we had put forth a lot of effort for just a tiny reward.

We were wrong. As we made breakfast, the kids came to us, telling the story of a UFO that had landed close by in the middle of the night, and they each claimed to have seen it. They came in a steady progression, the same kids that we had tried so hard to wake the night before. They hauled us out to the meadow to see the scorch marks left by the UFO. We found some odd-shaped metal disks and explained to the group that they were radiation detectors. They began further investigations and eventually roped off a small area, claiming that it was highly radioactive. According to the kids, the aliens had arranged some sticks in a secret message and left them there.

Amazingly, the adventure that so nearly failed was suddenly the most spectacular event of the camp session. The kids went back to the main camp and shared their phenomenal story over and over with the rest of the campers. Of course we supported their story, but no one was too sure whether to believe us or not. However, we were beginning to believe the story ourselves. For a time at least, we had left reality and were thoroughly caught up in our own adventure. We were the characters in a supremely grand story.

Our experience with the UFO adventure proved what we knew was true—kids love stories. And more than anything kids love to be inside the stories; they long to be part of the action. When a story is lived out, it becomes an adventure. So we started creating adventures that kids could live. Adventure's foundational element is fun. Real fun has been lost from most of society. Real fun is not the "responsible fun" of adulthood; real fun is the unadulterated fun of childhood. It is fun without worry or fear or the need to impress others. A child's fun has no social radar. A child has fun no matter who is watching or listening. When a child plays, there is no outside world. And when we watch children play, we smile and feel good. So why can't we return, at least for a while?

Good Stories, Good Games

Is there anything more captivating than a good story—you know, the kind that grabs us and takes us away from the immediacy of life for a while? The only trouble with such stories is that we, as readers or listeners, are not included. Why can't we be the detectives, the archaeologists, or the sharpshooters? Why can't we hop the next freight train to Carson City, or fly as lead pilots in the greatest air battle ever fought?

When Steve Torrey was very young, he was captivated by Peter Pan. To Steve the dream of flying to other lands was not just a dream; it was a possibility. Thinking that fairy dust came from the wings of moths, he ran around the yard catching the unfortunate creatures and rubbing them on his arms. He was so convinced that fairy dust would make him able to fly that he was terribly disappointed when it didn't.

In an adventure game there are no such disappointments. All that we imagine can come true on the playing field. No matter how many people are playing the game, all will have their own pages—or even chapters—in the story.

Everybody Needs a Hero

At the end of every story is a hero, someone you come away loving. At the end of every adventure game there are many heroes. They are the players in your adventure—all of them. Before we give the final scores or take showers or eat goodies, we take some time to let our heroes reminisce aloud. Whether they talk about almost reaching the goal or having the treasure just within their grasp, they will all have experienced an adventure and have loved it.

Finding the Right Story

Don't be disturbed if you do not have millions of stories floating around in your head waiting to be turned into games. Not all of our ideas are completely original; we constantly borrow from history, geography, science, literature, and television. One of the games in this book was an offspring of James Fenimore Cooper's *Leather-Stocking* Tales. Another was inspired by *The Goonies*, a popular Steven Spielberg film. And the adventure game *Get Smart* (Chapter Three) borrows more than just its name from the old TV show. For every battle fought, every territory pioneered, every treasure hunted, a game is waiting to be invented.

Using a Story

Stories are the foundation upon which adventure games are built. Story-plus-game-equals-adventure: it's as simple as that. It's important to really live the stories that make up our adventures. So when we play spy games, we put on trenchcoats and dark glasses, dim the lights, and speak in hushed voices. For other games our disguises are more flamboyant. We paint our faces in bright colors and storm through the woods with whoops and war cries. Costume, setting, and acting all add to the thrill of the adventure.

Game leaders set the example. If players are expected to "go into battle" fully dressed, we can't give them battle instructions wearing t-shirts and shorts. Encourage the spirit of the game. Be a gangster. Be a bushman. Be somebody.

Rules of the Game

In this book we repeat the rules twice for each game—first in a basic, outline form for easy reference, and then in the context of the story that we tell our players. We weave the rules right into the story so that the players are drawn into the adventure from the very beginning. You may use these stories as scripts or just add their flavor to your own dramas.

We also make sure that the rules are given in a setting that fits the overall mood of the game. In *Get Smart* (Chapter Three), for example, we dim the lights and have a couple of thugs escort the rules-giving agent to his post. We have included many suggestions for realistic settings that will grip your players from the outset of the game.

Extra Hints for Organizers

The better your story is, the better your game will be. And the more time you spend developing the story line, the more time you will have to watch the players act out the story. And never be afraid to get completely involved. Your excitement will catch on!

The fewer rules you have, the less chance there is for confusion. And although the rules are simple, the game itself will seem intricate. Bounty Run (Chapter Eleven) has only five basic rules, but the search for treasure can carry the players through hours of fun.

The fewer rules an adventure game has, the more set-up time it will typically require. There is an inverse relationship between the number of rules and the time it takes to set up a game. So if your preparation time is limited, you may not want to run a treasure hunt that has few rules but requires you to create a lot of clues and discover many places in which to stash treasures. When you can take the time to prepare intricacies in a game, however, it pays off, and your players will get caught up in the story.

CHAPTER TWO

What Goes into a Really
Great Game

WE BEGAN CREATING NEW ADVENTURE GAMES in response to a very real need, the need to divert the energies of our campers away from a highly successful game that we had already created—Outpost. Outpost was more than an adventure game—it was an event. And it soon took over the minds, energies, and imaginations of all its players.

We didn't plan it that way. In fact for about eight summers, we were amazed at the popularity of Outpost at our camp. We played other more typical games, but Outpost was the big event. Kids arrived at camp with full outfits of army fatigues. Many had tubes of face paint packed in with their sleeping bags and bug repellent. It was actually a little scary. A tradition larger than Outpost? There was no such thing.

In spite of all this enthusiasm, problems eventually developed. A handful of kids claimed that they came to camp just to play the game—and they were disappointed because we only played the game once during each three-week session. Before long we had a good sized bunch of Outpost maniacs on our hands. These enthusiasts worked hard to twist the rules of Outpost in their favor. Soon the game became just too competitive; the spirit of adventure had been lost.

And so we were driven to design different types of adventure games simply because of the popularity of Outpost. We knew that if we created games similar to Outpost, we could retain the element of adventure while at the same time minimize the element of competition. If we created enough adventure games, we figured, and played each one only a couple of times, none of the kids would have a chance to get good enough at the strategy to become especially competitive. The plan worked.

As we developed more adventure games, we began to think about the entire process of creating adventure. It's not as easy as it sounds and it's important to learn the basics first. In this chapter we give you the basics—plus lots of practical suggestions for running the best adventure game you possibly can.

Types of Games

Adventure games are called wide games because they demand more space and usually more time than typical group games. In general there are only three types of wide games—chase games, capture games, and hunt games. All of our games are variations or combinations of these three.

Chase games are glorified tag games. Members of one team chase members of another team (or teams), trying to capture prisoners or eliminate them from the game. Although there is usually more than just a simple chase going on, most adventure games use the chase in some part of the game.

In capture games, one team attempts to steal an object (or objects) from the opposing team. These objects are not hidden; instead, they are protected by people, space, or both. Capture the Flag is a good example of a capture game that also incorporates elements of the chase.

Hunt (or treasure hunt) games are similar to capture games in that two teams are attempting to capture an object, but in hunt games the treasure is hidden. Only the game's organizers know where the treasure is.

Hunt games involve the greatest amount of set-up time because the organizer must lay out the entire hunt, including developing the maps or clues that guide players to a certain goal or prize. If you have a strong story line, you have the perfect opportunity for a treasure hunt. And you'll find that the adventure the players get out of it is well worth the effort you put into it.

There are three ways to organize a hunt game. The simplest way is to have both teams race toward the same treasure. The problem with this method is that one team may follow the other team, rather than try to find the treasure using the clues. A second way that we have found to be more fair than the first is to establish two similar hunts with separate treasures. Both teams get a treasure, and the team that has more effectively worked through its clues gets there first. This second method demands more of the game's organizer, but really makes for a more judicious hunt. The final way lies somewhere between the first two possibilities; there is only one treasure, but there is more than one route by which to find it. Bounty Run (see Chapter Eleven) uses this final method.

The second and third choices also present a problem. How do you know that your hunts are of equal difficulty?

Actually you probably won't know, but you also most likely won't be able to guess correctly which team will find its treasure first. We've had an extremely poor record of predicting which hunt is the hardest, and, although this poor record may be a peculiarity, it has assured us that our hunts are fair. (An extra hint here: we have often used two organizers to set up different treasure hunts. Each organizer then runs through the other's hunt to identify any gross inequalities or snags.)

The final matter to consider is the ability of your team leaders. Do not put all of the good leaders or good treasure seekers on the same team. And remember, athletes may not always be the best leaders. Those who like to work puzzles or who can logically think their way through tricky problems may work better as leaders in hunt games.

Game Organizers and Leaders

Your job as game organizer is to prepare the game and to make sure it runs well. But in adventure games, there is a difference between leaders and organizers. Organizers run the game; leaders play it.

Tactically, leaders usually determine the overall team strategy. In some cases leaders are not on the teams, but instead play against the teams as a neutral hindrance to all players.

Leadership is not simply a matter of position, it is a matter of perspective. The leaders in any game need to be motivators but not muscle men. They should be adventurers, grown-up dreamers who know how to be as creative as possible within the rules. But they should not be so intent upon winning the game that they seek every possible way to stretch or squeeze the rules to their team's advantage. Instead, a truly good leader will clarify rather than question the rules and will tone down petty competition, encouraging, instead, the fun of the whole adventure.

How Many Can Play?

All this talk about leaders and players brings up an important question—how many people can play an adventure game? Actually this may depend on the size of your playing field or on the nature of your game. Most of the games in this book are designed for about sixty players, but almost all of them can be adapted to accommodate larger or smaller groups.

To adjust the game to the size of your group, you need to modify the size of the playing area. We have been fortunate to set up some of our games on many, many acres of thick forest, but we also realize that some groups simply don't have that much space. A smaller playing region works for most of our adventure games, especially when fewer people are playing.

Choosing a Playing Site

When deciding on a site, remember that terrain and cover are more important than size. A small area that is thickly wooded works better for some games than a vacant lot three times its size. When we play some of our games, we have the advantage of a large forest, as well as a creek whose pools and falls have served as everything from pirate coves to swimming holes. But many of these games can be played just as well in city parks, on college campuses, or even in city business districts.

The important thing is to match the playing site with a suitable story line. Meadows and forests can easily be transformed into the frontiers, jungles, and jail yards needed in hunt games; a city setting works best for spy games, and rolling hills and valleys are perfect for military games.

How Long Do We Play?

The games in this book are designed to last anywhere from forty-five minutes to four or five hours. The important principle to keep in mind is that the adventure should be just short enough that the players beg for more. It's better to have a game that is too short than too long.

If we plan to play a game for four hours and the target or goal is reached in eighty minutes, we don't stop the game unless we're ready to do so. Instead, we restore lives, reassign leaders, and do everything we can to keep the game rolling without admitting that the game is starting over. To announce that the game is starting over robs from the team that has accomplished its goal the satisfaction of winning. But to say that the game is being extended gives the winning team a chance to "do it again." (We are also giving the other team an opportunity to win as well, but we don't advertise that fact too loudly!)

Many of the games in this book do not end automatically, even if the treasure is discovered or the chief goal is attained. As the organizer, you can determine the lengths of these games. If nightfall comes sooner than expected and you need to finish before dark, you may quit as dusk settles in. If one team is defeating the other but the players are enjoying the game, you may lengthen the adventure to allow the trailing team a chance to catch up. The time frame of the game is flexible—to just keep having fun is the main objective.

It is difficult to predict the time that will be involved in a hunt game. If a treasure hunt is too difficult, the players may be stumped by the clues. If this happens, give the treasure seekers a bit of help. After all, the goal of a treasure hunt is to find the treasure! Just make sure that each team gets the same information.

And sometimes a team will find a treasure sooner than you want. In most hunt-and-capture games (like Bounty Run), one team may steal from the other, so the game may continue even if many of the treasures have been found. As a matter of fact, the most exciting Bounty Run game we ever had occurred when one team captured a major treasure before the dinner break and tried to guard it until the game's end. And guess what—they couldn't do it!

A Cease-fire Picnic

What's all this about a dinner break? We always allow for a break in our longer games. Dinner is a great excuse for a break, especially because we generally play our games during the summer when we can still put a couple of hours of hard play in after the meal.

24

There are several advantages to taking a break in the middle of a game. First, it allows the players to take a physical respite and begin swapping stories. Second, a break offers team leaders the chance to conduct small meetings with their players to re-evaluate strategy and player assignments. Finally, the break permits the organizers to evaluate the status of the teams and the players. We often give players extra "lives" at the break, or we give team leaders important hints if hunts are lagging behind schedule. We recommend that you schedule a break in all games that last more than four or five hours.

The Real Thing

If you want your story to become a real adventure, you should use props that are as authentic as possible. Your supplies should at least look like the real thing! Take the time to stain treasure chests and paint Jolly Rogers on the lids. Use weakly strung banjos to identify gambler roosts and flowing headdresses to mark Indian meeting grounds. You just can't be too real. (Check out garage sales and junkyards. They are great places to find props!)

And don't forget to use authentic costumes whenever possible. You may not be able to supply all your players with fatigues, loincloths, or bush wear, but do what you can. Also, encourage the players to round up workable but realistic gear.

A Few Extra Hints for Organizers

Be original. We cannot emphasize this point enough. Don't rely unwaveringly on the rules and guidelines in this book. After all, we did not know the size or experience of your group when we devised the rules. You and you alone must make your game the adventure it is meant to be.

There are no copyrights on field games as there are on board games. Borrow freely from other game organizers (yes, that includes us!). If it helps build your confidence, use other people's material as much as possible. Of course, the more often you organize games, the more easily you will create your own adventures. The more willing you are to be original, the more satisfied you will be when your game becomes a classic adventure at the hands and in the minds of your players.

Be confident. Whereas being confident about your ability to create a game is important, confidence in running a game is critical. You need to feel secure in your leadership abilities. Game organizers are called upon to make decisions that affect the strategy, course, and sometimes even the outcome of the game. If you give players wishy-washy responses when they question the structure of the game, they will find it easier to stretch or abuse the rules. And the more readily the rules can be bent, the more readily they will be bent—which means that there will be more disputes to settle during the game.

No matter how much time you take, no matter how carefully you've planned your game, your players will ask you questions that you never expected. So brainstorm. Talk to others about your game before you play it. Have others help you identify the possible pitfalls of your game.

Even if you bounce your ideas off of a hundred other people, you will leave some base uncovered. And probably the one trouble spot you forget will be picked apart by a strategy-minded player. At that moment you must exude confidence. Quickly and fairly come up with an answer (even if it means creating a rule on the spot) that satisfies the inquirer's mind. Let the players believe that you have given that particular issue hours of thought.

Never let questions get out of hand. We once ran across a camper who had a knack for questioning everything. The only problem with young Judd's questions was that they never seemed to belong to the realm of possibility. Judd would ask, "What happens if you're taking your prisoner into the safe zone and while you're on the way you have to go to the bathroom, which is inside—and you have to get special permission to go inside—and someone from the other team steals your flag while a rattlesnake begins to cross your path?" You could end up answering questions like this all day long! Be firm in answering the important questions, and then get on with the game. It is fine to clarify rules, but let the players with repeated questions and awkward variations stay behind if they think they need to know more. Remember, the idea is to have fun, and if you suddenly find yourself turning into Professor McGame, then it's time to halt the lecture and send your players out to have the time of their lives.

Keep things simple. Rules should shape the course of your game, but they should not be so outlandish that they are forgotten or rejected on the playing field. Some of our games have quite long lists of rules. But these rules are simple, progressive, and leave little room for interpretation. The more flexible the rules are, the more difficulty there will be in controlling the game, and it can easily become a worthless free-for-all. The key issue is not the number of rules, but how the rules are presented. Make sure they are easily understood by the players and easily enforced by the organizer.

Plan ahead. If you have never organized a game before (and even if you have), be sure to give yourself plenty of time to prepare the game, especially if you are preparing a hunt game. We have always found it helpful to meet with our team leaders as early as twenty-four hours ahead of game time. This allows them time to look for gaps in our planning, begin preparing strategy, and ask questions that are important for their own preparation. They may also want to prepare their team members before the game, a process that helps build enthusiasm and takes care of a lot of those silly questions. If you have created your own game, this early get-together is especially important.

When you are playing a game for the second or third time, you will find that the preparation will become easier. For one thing, you can probably use the same props and supplies that you gathered earlier.

Keep the game fun. As you read through this book, you will feel the excitement that playing these games can develop. As we experienced with Outpost, occasionally this excitement gets a little out of control and a spirit of competition takes charge. These games can be made fun again easily by following a few suggestions:

*No one dies. No player should be knocked out of the game and forced to sit on the sidelines. If players lose one role, they should be able to continue playing in another sort of role. In Safari, for example, when the players who have the roles of the wild animals are killed, they can become wild headhunters who in turn can plague those on the safari. And in Outpost the most irritating opponents are the scouts, players who have lost the ability to kill or be killed and who then have the power to walk freely among the enemy. The only time players might be removed from action is if they are taken to jail, but even then they must be given a chance to escape. If a player is to be eliminated from play altogether, it should only be the result of some unacceptable action, not because of the game's rules.

Distribute leaders evenly. You should try to have a balance of leaders on each team. These can be people who have played the game before or who have a knack for hunting, chasing, or deducting. They may be counselors or older, more experienced players. They need to be able to quickly develop a strategy for the game from the list of rules they receive.

Allow plenty of time for players to talk about their experiences. This cannot be stressed too much. There are too many little victories that take place to let them go without applauding them. In each game, there are many ways to earn points also. Take the time to acknowledge individuals who have performed special feats. If you let the players talk about their experiences and then acknowledge the individuals who achieved special feats, by the time you announce the final scores, they will not matter so much, and everyone will feel good about the way the game went.

Make the most of your story line. We added a pregame parade of warring factions to Outpost. All the players marched to United Nations Peace Central as a rousing John Philip Sousa march played, and an arbitrator dramatically pled with them for peace. The participants felt it was a real war, but they knew it was only going to be a fun game.

CHAPTER THREE

Get Smart

GET SMART IS A SPY GAME that must be played at night. It lasts thirty to sixty minutes. The goal of *Get Smart* is for a large group of players to smuggle microfilm from one secret headquarters to another without being caught.

Teams and Players

Get Smart is played by two groups, KAOS and Control. KAOS is made up of kids; Control consists of leaders. The KAOS group should be about six times larger than the Control group. Players in the large KAOS group may be split into different teams, but all KAOS agents should be working together against the Control guards and not against each other.

Get Smart may be played by any number of people, but there should be one guard for every six or seven KAOS agents. Two neutral people are needed to help run this game—one stationed at the final goal (the KAOS headquarters) to collect microfilm as it is turned in, and the other at a site designated as the developing lab.

Stuff You Need

Small pieces of film. We use pieces of an old discarded movie as microfilm. You can also use small but heavy pieces of paper (tickets work well). You need about five pieces of microfilm for each player.

Flashlights. Each guard should have one flashlight to use as a ray gun.

Cups or small containers. These will be used as film collection bins that are located at KAOS headquarters. They should be marked so that there is a different container for each team of KAOS agents.

Heavy ink marker. The person stationed at the developing lab uses a marker to "develop" the film.

Portable flashing red light. This is used to identify KAOS headquarters. You can use any light that is bright enough to be spotted from twenty or thirty yards but won't illuminate the area around it. The light must turn off and on easily since it is not kept on during the entire game.

Control ID tags. These tags may be poker chips, metal slugs, golf tees, or any similar small objects. You need twice as many ID tags as there are KAOS agents. These tags will be divided equally among the Control guards (about ten per guard).

Secretly mark three sets of tokens to distinguish them from the others. Give one special set to the Control guard acting as Maxwell Smart (the wacky star of the TV show *Get Smart*), another set to the Control guard acting as Agent 99 (Smart's wife), and the third set to the player acting as Chief (the head of the Control division).

Searchlight (optional). We use a spotlight to search the area periodically during the game. Combined with a siren and some funny *Get Smart* sounds or voices, the spotlight makes the game more realistic and suspenseful. The spotlight does not stop players from moving, but it can help them see their enemies.

Story and Rules

The *Get Smart* story is best told in a room dimly lit by one or two beams directed at the narrator. Only KAOS agents are present at this meeting. The narrator enters as the theme music from the TV show *Get Smart* begins to play. He is a shadowy figure dressed in a trenchcoat, stocking cap, and dark glasses. Speaking in a low-pitched voice, the narrator maintains a sinister air throughout the tale.

"I am Agent 47. I work for KAOS, but I also work for Control. I am a double agent. As KAOS agents you have been assigned to help me carry out an important KAOS mission. You will need to wear dark clothing and darken your faces. You have ten minutes to change and come back here."

When we play this game as a camp activity, we give the kids this introductory information and send them back to their dormitories to change. If you are planning to use this game as an event for your youth group, include information about how to dress in pre-event flyers and have the kids come in costume. When the players return, the agent begins again.

"Agent 47 here again. We at KAOS have uncovered an extraordinary new energy source. If sold on the world market, it would generate billions of dollars.

"This new energy source was first discovered when the Amefab [a name we made up] nuclear reactor exploded not too long ago. Our KAOS spies moved in to investigate; so did agents from Control. During their investigation KAOS spies unearthed the plans for Proton Hydrocosmic Atomic Radioactive Tension. These plans were microfilmed by KAOS Agent 22 while clean-up at the power plant was taking place. Until Agent 22 uncovered these plans, no one but a few Amefab experimenters knew anything about this new energy source. Unfortunately, Agent 22 has been kidnapped by Control. The Control guards demagnetized his tracking device, and we have lost all contact with him. What is even more unfortunate is that the microfilm of the plans is now in the hands of Control. We must get it back!

"Right now Control is storing this microfilm in their lab. Through my work as a double agent, I have been able to gain access to the Control lab tonight for just forty-five minutes. You KAOS agents must get inside and carry out the microfilm. Carry as many pieces of microfilm from the Control lab to our headquarters as you can, but because of the danger involved, carry only one piece at a time. The location of Control headquarters is the volleyball court [or any other place you select]. We will meet there at the appointed time.

"If you choose, you may take your microfilm to the KAOS developing lab before taking it to headquarters. At this point, Control does not have the technology to process our microfilm, so it is still undeveloped. The film will be more valuable if you bring it to us developed but taking the time to have this done does pose serious risks. The film developing lab is under the girls' cabin [or whatever place you choose]. If you go there, the developer will process your film and you can then proceed to KAOS headquarters. Remember—it is not imperative to have your film developed—it is just more valuable to us if you do.

"You must bring the film, developed or undeveloped, to the temporary KAOS headquarters. The headquarters can be recognized by a flashing red light. This light may not always be on and our headquarters' location has been kept a secret because there is always the threat of a major counterattack. At the headquarters a KAOS agent will collect your film. Make sure that you tell him which team of agents you are working with so that he puts the film in the right processing bin; you don't want your bonus given to someone else! After you deliver your film, you may return to Control headquarters and I will give you more.

"This whole mission may sound simple, but there is danger involved. Control guards are always protecting the area around their film lab to keep intruders away. These guards are armed with ray guns. [Yes they are really flashlights, but the KAOS agents don't need to know that now.] If you are zapped by a ray gun, freeze and act innocent. When the Control guard comes over and asks you to give him your microfilm, go ahead and do so. The guard's ray gun has exposed the film making it useless, but he doesn't know that.

"While you give your film to the guard, no one can harm either of you. The guard cannot zap any other agent, and no agent may sneak up on him. Always surrender on the spot to a Control guard. If you do not, Control will terminate you and you will be knocked out of the mission completely. Those are direct orders from the top!

"If you lose your microfilm to a Control guard, return immediately to me at the Control lab and I will give you more. No use crying over spoiled film.

"We are willing to give you bonuses for stolen Control ID tags. Here's how to get them—the ray guns carried by the guards are some of their weakest weapons; they can remain on for only three seconds and then must be shut off and recharged for five seconds. If you can sneak up and tag a Control guard during this five-second period or any other time when the guard cannot see you, the guard will be forced to turn over an ID tag to you. Keep that tag with you and turn it in for a bonus at the end of the mission.

"When you steal an ID tag from a guard, that guard is momentarily powerless and must let you escape into the darkness. The guard will then go back to protecting Control territory and you should resume your mission. When a guard's ID tags are all gone, that guard's ray gun is unusable until more ID tags are obtained from another guard. If it is possible and you enjoy risk-taking, you may steal ID tags from more than one guard on any mission.

"Some Control guards are special agents, and their ID tags are worth more at the end of the mission. There are even rumors that Maxwell Smart himself is guarding the Control lab.

"Let me repeat a few essential instructions. You must turn in the film to KAOS headquarters to receive your bonus. Keep any ID tags you steal until the mission is complete. If you are hit by a Control ray beam, surrender your film and return to Control headquarters. We'll be heading toward those headquarters in just a minute.

"The mission is over when you hear the bell (or whatever signal you use). Report back here after the mission."

After these instructions and before you begin the game, you will need to answer any questions that the players may have and also identify the physical boundaries of the game.

Rules and Advice for Guards

When you go over the rules with the guards, you do not need to tell them the story although you may choose to do so. Whatever you decide be sure to stress the following rules to the guards.

Site locations. There are three important locations— the Control headquarters, the KAOS headquarters, and the KAOS developing lab. Only the location of Control headquarters should be revealed. If guards discover the other locations, they

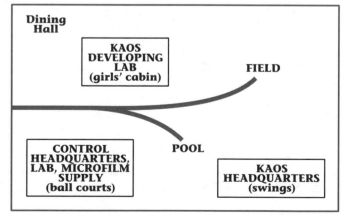

should police them from a distance of twenty yards or more.

Using ray guns. A guard's job is to keep KAOS agents from smuggling microfilm out of Control's film lab and into KAOS headquarters. They can do this using their ray guns (flashlights). Guards may keep their ray guns on for three seconds, but then they must turn them off for five seconds. If they catch a KAOS agent in their radar gun's beam, they can command the agent to freeze and collect that agent's film.

ID tags. The Control guards are each given approximately ten ID tags. KAOS agents may steal the ID tags by tagging the Control guards. If a guard is tagged, that guard must give up an ID tag to the tagging KAOS agent. The KAOS agent must then be given a free run back into the darkness.

Guards who run out of ID tags during the game need to get more from other guards since their ray guns are inoperable until they get more ID tags.

After explaining the rules you should also identify the game's physical boundaries.

Remind your guards that this is the kids' game to win, and as KAOS agents, the kids are the ones who will be earning team points. While guards need to get into the game's spirit, they never earn points.

The guards are responsible for keeping the game fast paced, so they may need to let some kids go even if they spot them. This is especially the case if you are playing *Get Smart* on a night when the moon is bright.

The End and the Score

You could play *Get Smart* for hours and many would still beg to play longer. We have found that forty-five minutes seems to be the perfect duration for this game.

When you have signaled for the game to stop and players return to the meeting place, give them time to tell stories about their adventures. This is fun for them and lets you see how they are reacting to the game. You may make changes the next time you play based on the things you hear from participants.

Tally the scores after about twenty minutes of story swapping. Take some time to recognize players who have earned points in various ways for their teams. If you are playing *Get Smart* as one of many events, you may need to adjust our score allotments. If this is the only game you will play, the scoring chart below should work very well.

Only microfilm delivered to the KAOS headquarters before the signal ending the game is counted toward team points. Collect stolen Control ID tags from players, sort them into the correct team containers, and award points for them as well. When the scoring is complete, players may enjoy keeping extra film or ID tags as souvenirs.

Scoring Chart
Undeveloped film .... 1,000 points
Developed film .... 3,000 points
Control guard ID tag .... 4,000 points
Agent 99 ID tag .... 8,000 points
Maxwell Smart ID tag .... 10,000 points
Chief ID tag .... 14,000 points

Give an additional 5000 points to any team turning in more than 25 pieces of microfilm.

Extra Hints for Organizers

For this game to be a success, darkness is essential. The more light that shines on or around the playing area, the more difficult it becomes for KAOS agents to complete their mission—and the game already favors the guards because they are allowed to carry flashlights. You may need to turn off any outdoor lights before play begins. The light from the moon can also have an adverse effect on the game. If you can play *Get Smart* on a night when there is little or no moon or when the moon is late in rising, you'll be in great shape.

You can always add interesting spy-oriented elements to *Get Smart*. As an organizer, you can devise some meaningless secret message (like, "The rain in Spain stays mainly in Des Moines") to say to players during the game. Don't tell the players that this is a secret message. After the game allow players to come up to you and tell you the secret message. If no one tells you, ask if any player knows the secret message. If any of them can repeat the phrase, give them 5000 points.

Get Smart for Older Players

If you plan to play this game with older players, some simple changes make the game more sophisticated. You may find that teams do not work very well (unless you are playing dorm versus dorm, or floor versus floor). If you don't have teams—and maybe even if you do—you can choose to eliminate captured players from the game instead of allowing them to return for more microfilm and another start. If this is the case, mark a circle on the back of each player's right hand. When a guard catches a player, the guard puts a large "X" through the circle. The game ends when all the players have been eliminated or have reached the KAOS headquarters. You may have to alter the story a bit, and you'll probably want to get rid of the developing lab.

Creativity is the key to making *Get Smart* the adventure of a kid's lifetime. Don't hesitate to change the story line or the game's make-up to fit your individual situation. After all, you must be feeling pretty creative by now!

Get Smart: Outline of Rules

Scenario
KAOS agents attempt to smuggle microfilm out of Control headquarters.

Playing Time
Forty-five minutes at night.

Stuff You Need
small pieces of film
flashlights
cups or small containers
one heavy ink marker
a portable flashing red light
small tokens (e.g., tickets) as ID tags

Characters
Leaders are Control guards.
Players are KAOS agents.

Object
Players earn points in one of two ways:

1. They smuggle secret microfilm strips from Control headquarters to KAOS headquarters.

2. They ambush Control guards and confiscate their ID cards.

The KAOS Mission

1. To begin the game, each KAOS agent receives one strip of undeveloped microfilm at Control headquarters.

2. KAOS agents try to avoid Control guards' ray beams while sneaking through the playing area to KAOS headquarters.

3. If KAOS agents reach their headquarters without being hit by a ray beam,

they turn in their film to the KAOS agent in charge of the headquarters.

4. After turning in their microfilm, KAOS agents return freely to Control headquarters, get another strip of microfilm, and make another attempt.

5. KAOS agents may tell other KAOS agents the location of their headquarters, but if there are competing teams within KAOS, players should tell only their teammates.

6. For added points, KAOS agents may take their undeveloped microfilm to the "film lab" before taking it to KAOS headquarters. Please note the following special rules about the film lab:

*The location of the film lab is known by game leader/narrator and is told only to KAOS agents.

*Control guards are not told the location of the film lab, but eventually will discover it. When they do, they must remain at least twenty yards away from it.

*KAOS agents making it to the film lab hold out their film so that it can be developed (marked with a marker pen) by the film developer.

*KAOS agents may then continue on to KAOS headquarters and turn in their developed film.

The Control Defense

1. Control guards have ray beam guns (flashlights), which are used to disable KAOS agents.

2. Control guards can have their ray beams on for a maximum of three seconds. They must then have them off at least five seconds for recharging.

3. During a three-second ray beam shot, it is possible for a Control guard to disable more than one KAOS agent.

4. When KAOS agents are hit by a ray beam, they must stop; they cannot run away.

*KAOS agents must then surrender microfilm (undeveloped or developed) to the Control guard.

5. Control guards may leave their flashlights on during this transaction to help obtain the microfilm, but they may not use them to look for or to disable other KAOS agents.

If a KAOS agent disabled by a Control guard has an ID tag obtained from a previous ambush, the tag does not have to be surrendered—only the microfilm strip.

6. When a Control guard hits a KAOS agent with a flashlight beam and confiscates his microfilm, both parties are then free from further ambush for a five-second "scatter time."

7. After KAOS agents surrender their microfilm, they have free passage back to Control headquarters to get another strip of microfilm and begin the mission again.

8. If a KAOS agent refuses to stop or turn in microfilm, that agent is out of the game.

The Ambush

1. Control guards carry a supply of ID cards. Certain guards may be special characters (see Story and Rules).

2. A KAOS agent ambushes by tagging the Control guard.

*The tag cannot occur during a guard-agent transaction.

*An ideal time to tag is during the five-second recharging period following a three-second ray beam shot when no agent was disabled.

*Only one KAOS agent may ambush a Control guard at a time.

3. During an ambush transaction:

*The control guard gives one ID card to the KAOS agent who made the successful ambush.

*Both the Control guard and the KAOS agent are free from attack until after a five-second "scatter time" that follows the transaction.

4. When a Control guard loses all ID tags to ambushes, that guard may not

use a ray beam until at least one new ID tag is obtained. The ID tags may only be obtained from other Control guards.

Ending the Game

Get Smart ends with a loud signal at the end of the playing time. The scores are figured according to the scoring table.

CHAPTER FOUR

Safari

THE JUNGLE IS A MARVELOUS PLACE for an adventure. Unfortunately, the United States does not have much to offer in the way of thick bush, head-hunting natives, and big game. But Safari changes all that. Any wooded area can instantly become a jungle if you import a few animals and wild headhunters!

A daytime game that should be played on twenty to forty densely wooded acres, Safari is a big-game adventure where hunters track jungle animals and search for legendary tribal treasures. While the size of the playing site can vary, it should be thick with trees and bushes. A playing region with at least one creek or pool of water is a great setting for a Safari adventure.

Safari can be especially exciting if you have some group leaders who are real comedians. The group leaders or counselors can play the part of animals in the jungle, making loud cries and unpredictable attacks. The more the animals ham it up, the better the game.

Teams and Players

Safari pits two teams of players against one another in a big game hunt. Any number of people may play Safari, but you will need four or five hunters for every animal. If you have eight animals, for example, you would want forty hunters. The game organizer and assistants act as Safari suppliers and game wardens. Throughout the game, they are stationed at a central location, called the Safari Supply Station.

Stuff You Need

Different colored T-shirts. These are used to identify the various animals. They can be supplied by the "animals" themselves, but you will need to tell each animal what color to wear. We usually play with six different animals—elephants, hippos, monkeys, tigers, lions, and snakes. Any combination of animals will work as long as each animal is identified by a different shirt color.

Socks partly filled with flour. We use socks partly filled with flour to represent snake venom. A snake has successfully bitten when its sock makes contact with a hunter.

Water weapons. An elephant uses water weapons to fend off hunters. These may be squirt bottles, water pistols, backpack fire extinguishers, or anything that can hold or squirt water.

"Watering holes." Hippos are safer from attack when they are waist deep in water. An ideal playing area will have a small lake, a slow moving stream, or a swimming pool. It's even more fun if there are several watering holes. Hippos are not completely safe in the water, but it is harder for them to be wounded there. If your playing area does not have any small bodies of water, consider some of the following alternatives:

*Rope off one or more areas, designate them as watering holes, and label them with creative names like Lake Hippowada, Zulu Swamp, or Kilimanjaro River.

*Set up several children's wading pools.

*Fill up plastic garbage cans with water.

*Set up a sprinkler. You can turn on permanent ones or use the kind that attach to a garden hose. The hippo is "safe" only when under the falling water. The sprinklers also will add a rain-forest effect to your game.

*Fill up flat plastic buckets (or storage bins) with water. To be safe, the hippo needs to stand in one of the buckets full of water.

Safari cards. Each hunter is given one preprinted card to carry during the game. Each card contains a chart explaining which animals are in the jungle, what color they wear, how to kill them, and how they defend themselves. You can make an original chart on an index card and then make enough photocopies to distribute it and still have extras on hand.

The safari card is essential to this game. Without it the hunter would have a difficult time identifying animals in the jungle. At the same time, the fact that the hunter must refer to the safari card gives the animals a bit of an advantage over the hunters. After all, part of the challenge of any safari is that the animals are more familiar with the jungle than the hunters.

Game warden's chalkboard. The information on the card is also placed on a chalkboard at the Safari Supply Station so that players may refer to it while the game rules are being reviewed. This information needs to be brief and in summary form. Here's an example:

This same board can be re-used during the game to keep a visible record of the snakebites, head shrinks, and animal kills that have been earned.

Safari Chart

Elephant (red) five wounds for kill. "E" guns only.

Hippo (white) four wounds for kill. "E" guns if out of water; four hunters must tag if hippo is in water.

Tiger (blue w/headband) three wounds for kill. Must tag on back; one team only may wound and kill.

Lion (blue) two wounds for kill. Must pull tail. Travel within one hundred feet of each other.

Monkey (green) two wounds for kill. Travel within seventy-five feet of each other; may climb trees.

Snake (dark color) one wound for kill. Possess dangerous snakebite defense.

Native (sash) secret number. Riddle to the Great Image.

Headhunter (sash and hood) may catch hunters and shrink their heads. Look out!

Good luck! It's a jungle out there!

Polaroid camera and backdrop (optional). With a Polaroid camera and a background pierced with a hole large enough for the animal to place its head through, you can take pictures of big game hunters with their "mounted" catches.

Envelopes containing "native numbers" and riddles. A secret number between one and five is given to each native. The numbers are written on paper, one number per envelope. Make up a riddle and enclose half of it in each envelope; every envelope contains either the first half or the second half of the same riddle.

For example, to lead hunters to The Great Image you have buried in a camp's fire circle, you could use this riddle.

> Sometimes I'm hot and very bright,
> You like me best when it is night.
> Right now I'm cold, and black you'll be
> By looking for The Great Image in me.

Give half of the natives the first part of the riddle (the first two lines), and the other half the second part (the last two lines).

The Great Image. This may be any small, symbolic object that can be used as a hidden treasure. We have used a marble egg as The Great Image. You may want to have a second Great Image on hand in case you need to lengthen the game.

A single-hole punch. A hole punch is used to mark the cards of hunters chosen by their team to carry elephant guns.

Poker chips or game tokens. These are given to the animals to be used as wounds.

Sashes and hoods. A simple strip of cloth may be worn around the waist as a sash. A rectangular piece of cloth tied with a string may serve as a hood (it will look much like the hoods desert nomads wear in old movies). These are used to transform the costume of an animal into that of a headhunter.

Story and Rules

You should give these rules to your animals well ahead of the time you wish to begin the game, hours to days in advance. Decide together who will play each animal (you can assign roles if necessary). If you prepare the animals beforehand, you will be able to begin playing Safari immediately after giving the rules to the hunters, because during that same time the animals can go out into the playing area and hide.

To give the rules for Safari, adopt the classic look of a big game hunter: khaki pants or shorts, green or khaki shirt, boots, an Aussie camouflage hat, binoculars strung about your neck, and a rolled up map in your hand. You could also hang netting, palm fronds, or thick ferns in the room. You could even deliver your rules sitting on top of a big wooden shipping crate. Remember to have a chalkboard on hand with the same instructions on it as are on the safari cards. Refer to this chalkboard as you describe the jungle animals.

"Good afternoon, folks. I hope you are enjoying your excursion to the bush of Africa. For many of you, this will be the greatest adventure of your life. All of the creatures you have seen on your television set will suddenly come to life—and they may also become your very own trophies. In a few moments I will tell you all you need to know for jungle survival, but first I want to whet your appetites for big game hunting by describing some of the ferocious beasts you will track.

"Mighty elephants may seem harmless creatures in the zoo or circus, but in the bush they are terrifying! Their method of defense is not deadly, but it will ruin your neat American haircuts and clothes because the elephants use their trunks to drench any who come close. You will be able to identify elephants by their red T-shirts. When an elephant has been wounded five times, he will die. Only those with powerful elephant guns may wound an elephant. The elephant and the hippo are the only animals that can be wounded by an elephant gun.

"The hippopotamus is an incredible beast that craves the coolness of water. A hippo can be identified by its white coloring and must be wounded four times before it will die. Outside of the water, the hippo is an easy target for those who are fortunate enough to carry elephant guns, but it is too large to be wounded by normal rifles. Because elephant guns do not work in water, they are no threat to a wallowing hippo."

Depending on how you have set up your watering hole, you may need to modify the following instructions.

"So when the hippo is waist deep in water, hunting gets a little bit tricky. A hippo may be wounded in the water only if it is tagged by four hunters simultaneously.

"Tigers are fast and ferocious beasts, armed with deadly claws and teeth. Tigers wear blue T-shirts and a headband. Use any gun to wound a tiger, but you must wound it three times in the back to kill it. Because tigers are swift, they are difficult to follow. So to keep the competition fair, once a team has wounded a particular tiger, the other team may not wound or kill that same beast. (Be sure each tiger finds out which team wounded it first.)

"If you see a lion in the jungle, another lion will always be nearby because lions travel in twos or threes, no more than a hundred feet apart. Lions wear blue. You can wound a lion by pulling its tail and need only to wound a lion two times to kill it, but remember that lions invariably are on the lookout for one another.

"If you hear a harsh cry coming from somewhere above you, it is the call of a monkey. Monkeys are clothed in green and they are hard to see in the trees. You need to wound a monkey just two times to kill it, but be warned that monkeys like to hang together and will always be within seventy-five horizontal feet of each other.

"The snakes are the sneakiest and most dangerous animals in the jungle. Snakes have excellent camouflage and may wear any dark color. Although just one shot kills a snake, these venomous reptiles have a dangerous bite. If you are bitten by a snake (hit with its flour-filled sock), the snake will bring you back to the safari supply station and a snakebite will be recorded against your team.

"You will all be given a safari card to carry with you in the jungle.

On it is a small rendition of the chart before you on this chalkboard. Your safari card will remind you of the colors animals wear, their methods of defense, and the number of wounds it takes to kill them. Do not lose this card; it is also your gun. To shoot an animal, you need only to tag it with your safari card. Once tagged, that animal will begin to count to ten out loud. Stay there. One of your teammates must tag the animal within that ten-second period. Then the animal is wounded.

"Your team will select seven players [or about a quarter of the team] to carry elephant guns. These players will have a special hole punched in their card permitting them to carry elephant guns.

"Now, some advice about safe travel in the jungle. You may go out in groups of any size, but never go out alone. If you are alone, you can be attacked by an animal—any animal. An animal attacks by tagging you and counting to ten. If no other hunter can get to the animal and wound it by the count of ten, the animal has wounded you, and will rip off one corner of your safari card. When all four corners have been ripped off, your gun is disabled and you must buy a new one at the supply station."

There should be no dispute about whether the animal or the hunter was tagged first. Either way, if a second hunter tags the animal within the ten-second period, the animal is wounded. If a second hunter does not show up, the hunter is considered wounded and must give up a corner of the safari card.

"You should not travel with members of the other team. If your team spots an animal first, you want an uncontested attempt at wounding it. You don't want members of the other team interfering. You also don't want to tell members of the opposition where you have seen certain animals.

"If you and a teammate both tag an animal before it counts to ten, you have shot the animal and get credit for wounding it. All animals carry special chips according to the number of wounds they may suffer. If you wound an animal, it will give you one of its wound chips. Carry this chip until the end of the game and then turn it in for points. These chips cannot be taken from you in any way during the game.

"Each animal has a limited number of wounds before it is killed. You will not know how many times an animal has been wounded unless you wound it for the last time. If the animal gives you its last chip, it will tell you that you have earned a kill. Even if you have not earned a kill, you still get credit for the wound, so turn the chip in at the end of the game. If you have earned a kill, bring the animal to the Safari Supply Station, and a kill will be recorded for your team. Each wound is worth points, but each kill is worth more points. You will not know whether you have killed an animal or simply wounded it until you and another hunter on your team have tagged the animal.

"There is one more important thing you must know about shooting animals. No animal can be wounded twice in a row by either of the two hunters involved in a wounding. Hunters may wound the same animal more than once, but not twice in a row. All animals who have been wounded must be given a free run back into the wild after they have given up a wound chip to the hunter.

"But there is more than big game to hunt in the jungle. When an animal has been returned to the Safari Supply Station, it is not knocked out of the game. Instead, that animal becomes a tribal native. Natives wear sashes around their waists and carry a piece of a riddle that can lead your team to The Great Image—the long-lost treasure of this tribal people that they have been searching for with their clues for some time.

"If you tag natives, attempt to guess their secret numbers. Each secret number is a number between one and five, and known only to its holder. If you guess their numbers correctly, the natives must give you their pieces of the riddle. Do not lose these. Even if you do not find The Great Image, turn in all riddle pieces for points at the end of the safari. If you do not guess a secret number correctly, you may not tag that native again—a native cannot be tagged by the same person twice. It is important to tell other team members about any natives you have tagged and any number(s) you have wrongly guessed. This way, the next person to tag at the native does not waste a guess.

"There are two pieces to the riddle, but there may be more than one copy of each piece since each native carries only one half. If you steal a piece to the riddle from one native, it will probably not be enough to find The Great Image. You will need to steal a second piece from another native. However this does not guarantee that the second piece will be different from the first. You may begin looking for The Great Image at any time, but it will be easiest to find when you have both halves of the riddle. No one knows what The Great Image looks like, but from the tales we have heard, it should be spectacular.

"If you find The Great Image, it is your responsibility to return it to the Safari Supply Station as quickly and quietly as possible. If you are tagged by a native or a wild headhunter, you will lose The Great Image, never to regain it. You may throw, pass, or hide The Great Image in your attempt to get it back to the supply station safely.

"Now you have just heard me speak of the wild headhunters. I wish I did not have to speak of them. The natives call them "the terrible people," for they are the most vicious creatures in all of the jungle, more terrifying than any tiger or snake you may encounter. And worst of all, they cannot be killed. These headhunters wear a sash as the natives do, but they also wear a hood. If you are tagged by one of these headhunters, you will be escorted back to the supply station where the headhunter will count you as a headshrunken victim and your team will lose points. Thanks to our doctors at the Safari Supply Station, you can never be taken out of the safari altogether. After a snakebite or a headshrink, we'll have you ready in no time to go right back out on the hunt. (A word of caution: due to postoperative techniques, people recovering from head-expansion operations have delusions that they are the greatest things alive.) You should know that these headhunters are natives who have lost their riddle pieces. So you see, the more animals that are killed, the more dangerous a place the jungle becomes for safari hunters! One more thing: you cannot have your head shrunk by the same wild headhunter twice."

Now take time to explain the physical boundaries of the game to the hunters. Then answer questions, have them meet with their teams to determine who will carry elephant guns, and distribute safari cards. Now you're ready for the jungle safari adventure of a lifetime!

Rules and Advice for Animals

You don't need to tell the story to the animals, but you may want to so that they get an overall feel for the game. Make sure that they have a thorough knowledge of all the rules. In a big game like Safari, your group's leaders—the animals in this case—are the ones who will need to control the game out in the wild. They should understand the rules well so they do not have to break the flow of the adventure by returning to the supply station to ask questions. Your leaders should be fair and they also should keep in mind the spirit of the game. Stress these facts and rules in your meeting with the animals.

Changing roles. Animals are never knocked out of the game. If you are killed as an animal, you become more active as a native and then most active as a headhunter.

Counting. Count at a normal pace. The animals can confound hunters by counting to ten at an unintelligible rate, but the ten-count is meant to cover ten seconds. You may want to ask them to count one-one thousand, two-one thousand, etc.

Participating actively. Hide but do not disappear. It is possible (especially if your playing area is very thick with foliage) to find a completely secluded spot and take a nap. Animals should not do this. The animals make this game an adventure; the more wild they are and the more they tease the players by being mischievous, the more exciting the game will be.

Traveling in groups. Make sure that animals who must travel together have partners. If one of the animals is killed and the other is not, the living animal may travel alone, but if it finds another (or others) of its kind, it should join the group.

Climbing trees. Only monkeys may climb trees. Any animal may go into the water, but only hippos find any protection there.

Clothing colors. Be sure that the different animals are wearing clothing of the appropriate color.

The End and the Score

Safari is one of the games that we play with a dinner break. If the riddle is sufficiently difficult (but not impossible), the game should last three or four hours before the hunters find The Great Image. If for some reason the image is found earlier, and particularly if it is found before any break you may be planning, you should have a second image already hidden and a matching riddle set on hand so that you can extend the game. You may end the game when The Great Image has been found, when time runs short, or when player morale dictates.

When you call the players together after the game, be sure to give them plenty of time to talk about their experiences. You may collect any wound chips and riddle pieces during this time, or you may wait until you have called for the player's attention and make a more dramatic "gathering of the spoils." If this is one game of many that you are playing, you may wish to adjust our scoring guide, but if this is the only game you will be playing, this score sheet should be usable.

Scoring Chart
Wounds of any animal ....1,000 points
Kills of monkeys or elephants..............5,000 points
Kills of hippos or snakes......................7,000 points
Kills of lions or tigers ....10,000 points
Riddle pieces ....15,000 points
The Great Image ....40,000 points
Snakebite antidote ....-1,000 points
Shrunken head surgery.......................-2,000 points

Extra Hints for Organizers

During the game keep careful records at the Safari Supply Station of several things—snakebites, shrunken heads, and animal kills. Players who are bitten by a snake should have a snakebite recorded against their team. Shrunken heads should be marked off in the same way. Last, any kills must be recorded according to the type of animal and the team that made the kill. The organizer also gives killed animals a sash to wear around their waist signifying that they have become natives, and cloth hoods to natives when they become headhunters. The organizer should give the riddle pieces to the natives in alternating fashion, with one half going to the first native, the other half to the second native, and so on.

You may want to place your chalkboard in front of the Safari Supply Station and use it to record any kills, snakebites, or shrunken heads for players to see as they come by the station. From this board, the players can get a good idea of how their team is doing throughout the course of the game.

Another fun idea is to have a Polaroid camera on hand, along with an old piece of paneling that has a head-sized hole cut in it. When a hunter brings in an animal after a kill, you can have the hunter pose with the "mounted" animal (which puts its head through the hole) and take an instant snapshot. You can then display the photographs at the end of a game to spur conversation.

Safari for Older Players

If you are playing Safari with an older, more competitive bunch, you may wish to add a twist to the search for The Great Image. Let the natives hunt for the image as well. Once they have obtained a riddle piece, they may use it to search for the ancient tribal treasure. This way, the natives may beat the hunters to the image. They could then sneak the image back to the Safari Supply Station, where it would be removed from the game. If you use this rule, you should not have the natives carry numbers. If they are tagged, they must forfeit automatically the riddle piece to the hunter. Of course, if the native has that riddle piece memorized, it is never really lost—and that native becomes a wild headhunter to boot!

Safari: Outline of Rules

Scenario
Big game hunters track and kill wild animals in the African bush.

Playing Time
Two to five hours.

Stuff You Need
different colored T-shirts
head bands
socks filled with flour
squirt guns or hoses
a single-hole punch
cloth hoods and sashes
watering holes
envelopes containing a number and a riddle piece
safari cards
chips or tokens
an item to act as The Great Image
chalkboard

Characters
Organizers are safari suppliers.
Leaders are wild animals, natives, and headhunters.
Players are big game hunters.

Object
Hunters may earn points in three ways:

1. They may wound and kill animals.

2. They may capture riddles from natives.

3. They may discover The Great Image, a prized native artifact.

Wounding and Killing Animals

1. Hunters use safari cards (see sample in this chapter) to identify various animals. Animals can be identified by the colors they wear.

2. Safari cards are also the hunters' guns. Some hunters receive elephant guns, which are marked by a hole punched in them.

3. Working as partners, two hunters tag an animal to wound it. If these hunters both tag the animal before it counts to ten, the hunters have wounded the animal and they receive a chip from the animal.

4. Special considerations:

*Lions must have their tail (a rag hanging from a back pocket) pulled to be wounded.

*Elephants and hippos may be wounded only by hunters carrying elephant guns.

*Snakes may "bite" hunters by hitting them with a flour-filled sock. Snakebitten hunters must go to the Safari Supply Station to be treated. These hunters also lose points.

5. No pair of hunters may wound the same animal twice in a row.

6. If one hunter tags an animal, or if an animal tags a hunter, and no other hunter tags the animal within ten seconds (counted by the animal), the hunter is wounded. The animal rips a corner off the hunter's gun. When all four corners have been torn off a hunter's gun, the hunter must buy a new gun from the safari suppliers.

7. Each animal dies after a certain number of wounds. If a pair of hunters inflict the final wound, the animal and hunters go to the safari suppliers where the hunters get credit for the kill.

Stealing Riddles from Natives

1. When animals die, they become natives and wear sashes around their waists to identify themselves. Natives also carry envelopes containing a number and a piece of a riddle.

2. Hunters tag natives and try to guess the number in the envelope. The number is between one and five. A hunter who guesses correctly receives the riddle piece, which may be turned in for points at the end of the game. A hunter who guesses incorrectly may not tag the same native again.

Wild Headhunters

1. Any native who loses a riddle piece becomes a wild headhunter. These headhunters wear the native sash and a hood.

2. Headhunters may freely tag game hunters. If a hunter is tagged, the headhunter brings the hunter to the safari suppliers, and the hunter loses points for having a shrunken head. The hunter may then return to play. One wild headhunter may not tag the same hunter twice in a game.

The Great Image

1. The riddle pieces are put together to form a complete riddle, a riddle that hints at the location of The Great Image.

2. Hunters may begin searching for The Great Image with only one piece of the riddle, but the riddle should be too difficult to decipher without both pieces.

3. If while using the riddle the hunters find The Great Image, they should return it to the safari suppliers without being tagged by a native or headhunter. If a hunter carrying The Great Image is tagged, The Great Image is lost for the rest of the game.

Ending the Game

The game ends when the organizers wish or when all the animals have become wild headhunters or when The Great Image has been found. The scores are figured according to the scoring table.

CHAPTER FIVE

Outpost

OUTPOST IS A COMBAT GAME requiring both strength and stealth. It is similar to the game Capture the Flag, only in Outpost the players are capturing players on the opposite team instead of a flag. Each member of the teams holds a different rank which carries a different point value. The ultimate goal of Outpost is to capture the opponent's generals, who are the players with the highest rank and value.

Outpost was one of the first games we invented, and it has become more and more sophisticated throughout the years. An additional chapter on Advanced Outpost (Chapter Six) follows, which adds the walkie-talkies to the basic game.

Teams and Players

Outpost is played by two teams, each with the same number of players. Any number of people may play Outpost. The older or more experienced players may be assigned leadership roles on their respective squads. Unlike the counselors and youth workers in *Get Smart* or *Safari*, leaders in Outpost are a part of the teams themselves. The organizer is the liaison between the two squads and throughout the game is stationed at a location that we call United Nations Peace Central.

Stuff You Need

Football flags or eighteen-inch cloth strips. You need one set of flags or one cloth strip per player. Each team should wear a different colored flag.

Player list. A list containing the names of all players from both teams is needed so that names can be checked off as captured players are brought to United Nations Peace Central by their captor. If you have a formal list of people in your group, you can use a copy of this list. If you do not have a list, players can sign in as they arrive at the game site.

Two sets of twenty index cards (forty total). Each set contains a different word from a twenty-word message in which no words are repeated, such as: "Enemy has scattered across the field to forty degrees latitude, but our forces have commenced response by setting wide flanks." These messages do not need to carry any particular meaning. They are used simply as a way of keeping scouts involved in the game by earning points for their team. Each field marshal takes ten of the cards given to his team.

United Nations Peace Central (UNPC). The UNPC will serve as a neutral site for players to report captures and turn in information cards. The UNPC may be indoors or outdoors, but it should be centrally located and accessible.

Four copies of the rules. Give one copy to each field marshal.

Chalkboard. This board is placed outside UNPC and is used as a collecting station for the code words turned in by various soldiers.

List of personnel and their ranks. Each Outpost team is made up of members with differing ranks and roles. The list below details these ranks from highest to lowest. In reviewing this list, keep in mind that the hierarchy of ranks is based on this simple principle: the higher the rank, the less lives a person has; and the higher the rank, the higher the point value a person has.

Generals. The generals are the most valuable officers on each team. They have one life. Generals are ranked according to the number of stars they have.

Field marshals. Field marshals are tacticians and they can neither capture other players nor be captured. As such, they cannot lose their lives. They are valuable to their team as strategists and valuable to the opponent as information holders.

Lieutenants. The lieutenants each have two lives and are the only active officers besides the generals.

Sergeants. Sergeants are the highest ranked real fighting men. Sergeants have three lives.

Infantry. The members of the infantry also have three lives, but they are of a lower rank than the sergeants and are worth fewer points. The majority of the fighting force should be infantry.

Scouts. The lowest ranking of all soldiers, scouts are those players who have lost all their lives. While scouts may not capture other soldiers, they may freely track opposing militia and steal information from field marshals.

Organizers. These participants are not active players but, instead, help at UNPC during the course of the game. This group will probably include you, the organizer, and one or two others interested in helping out.

Story and Rules

Outpost derives its story from a simple wartime confrontation. Because the organizer is a liaison between the warring parties, he gives the rules in the context of agreeing to govern the fighting during wartime. The organizer may be dressed in civilian or military attire, but should always be seen as neutral by both sides. Speaking with absolute authority, the organizer expresses the situation's seriousness.

"I am afraid that you soldiers are here for a reason very different from my own. If I could, I would stop this war! But you—you seem bent on using combat to decide which is the greater army. So although I believe you are mistaken, I have been called upon as mediator to establish the rules for this war. There will be stiff—do you understand me?—I said stiff penalties for those who do not abide by the rules.

"First, each soldier will be given a strip of cloth to wear in his back pocket. At least one half of the cloth must be hanging outside of that pocket, or below the bottom of your shirt if it is untucked. These strips of cloth may not be knotted, weighted, or tied in the pocket. They must simply be stuffed into the pocket. Any soldier violating this rule will forfeit all remaining lives and 10,000 points to the opposing army. [If you are using standard football flags, it is necessary only to say that the flags must be attached only as designed, and may not be wrapped around or tied to a belt.]

"Second, each soldier is given a rank by his army. Each team has five generals of different rank, two field marshals, two lieutenants, and five sergeants. The remaining soldiers are infantry. Generals begin the game with one life each. Field marshals may neither capture nor be captured. Lieutenants have two lives each. Sergeants and infantry have three lives each.

"Field marshals have an important role as strategists and rules advisors. Each field marshal will carry a set of rules. If you have a question about the rules, first ask one of your army's field marshals. You will lose a life if you come to UNPC and ask a question about a rule clearly stated in the rule book. Again, ask a field marshal first! [This rule will save you lots of trouble.]

"The five generals in each army are designated by star: five-star, four-star, three-star, two-star, and one-star. Because the generals are worth the greatest amount of points and because they have only one life each, I advise you to protect your generals carefully.

"You may try to capture soldiers of any rank. You do not need to know the rank of the soldier before attempting your capture. You may capture someone by pulling a flag off, but you may not hold or tackle your opponent in the process. Soldiers may not guard their flags with their hands, sit on their flags, or sandwich their flags with fixed objects, such as trees or buildings. The only way soldiers may protect their flags is by standing back to back or by running away.

"When you capture an opposing soldier, all other action ceases for you and that soldier. You may neither be captured nor capture another soldier. You must immediately decide whether to escort the prisoner to UNPC or to set the prisoner free. If you decide to escort the prisoner, you must head directly to UNPC where you will receive points for your capture. Both of you are safe from capture while en route.

"If instead you choose to let the prisoner go free, you must immediately give back the prisoner's flag and go elsewhere. No points are gained or lost.

"Generals may order other soldiers to escort their prisoners to UNPC, but all other soldiers are responsible for accompanying their own captives. Captured soldiers lose one of their lives. Soldiers who have captured others will be sent back to the front and may not pursue any soldier that they have just reported as captured. The game should not be played around UNPC. The practice of "leeching," or hanging around UNPC to capture other soldiers at any time, will cost you a life.

"Often two soldiers will claim to have captured each other's flag simultaneously. If these soldiers cannot decide who was tagged first, the dispute may be resolved in one of two ways. Each soldier may return the flag to its owner and the two may go their separate ways, agreeing not to chase one another. This type of truce costs neither soldier a life. Two soldiers may also bring their dispute to UNPC, but both soldiers will then forfeit a life and be sent back to the front.

"If a soldier (including a general) runs out of lives, that soldier becomes a scout. Scouts must tie their flags around their right wrists to designate their new rank. Although scouts may neither take lives nor be captured, they may track generals. [If you are playing the advanced version of Outpost, omit the following two paragraphs in your reading of the rules.]

"Scouts may also roam freely and attempt to steal information from opposing field marshals. To steal information from a field marshal, a scout must tag a field marshal on the back. The field marshal must then give the scout an information card to be returned to UNPC. A team receives 1,000 points for each information card it steals from a field marshal. Scouts must return one information card to UNPC before they may go back to seize another.

"Each team has two field marshals. Each field marshal has ten information cards with one word on each card. When the information cards are put together properly, they will form a twenty-word message. If a team unscrambles the message with complete accuracy, it receives 15,000 points. When cards are turned in to UNPC, the words found on them will be written on a chalkboard. Only scouts may attempt to unscramble the message.

"There are no time-outs. If you need to use a restroom, turn in your flag at UNPC. This puts you out of commission, and you may only rejoin the game after you have retrieved your flag.

"This war will be deemed as officially over when all five generals from one team have been captured or when a cease-fire has been called."

Now you need to identify the boundaries, specify any meal break, answer questions, and distribute supplies. At this point teams should be permitted to meet for about ten minutes to discuss soldier ranks and team strategies. When this period is over, the pageantry begins. While patriotic music booms, have players march before UNPC officials for a presentation of the troops. Each team submits its list of ranks and introduces its generals and field marshals.

The teams may then wish to demonstrate their comparative strength by a show of calisthenics. Afterwards the officials ask, "Is there any way that this issue can be resolved peacefully?" The standard answer is a boisterous "NO!" The officials then say, "This means WAR!" and send the teams in opposite directions. After five minutes, a bell is rung to signal the beginning of play.

The End and the Score

Outpost rarely ends by having all the generals captured. Signal the end of the game whenever you like, and, in fact, you may choose to continue the game even if all of one team's generals have been discovered.

Because soldiers report to the UNPC after every capture or acquisition of information, the only point gathering that must be done at the game's end is from soldiers who captured someone or something but could not return to report the spoils before the signal. As you wait for these soldiers and the others to return from the front, you may add up the scores you have already obtained and allow the soldiers to share their war stories.

If you are playing Outpost as a part of an overall competition, you may wish to revise our score sheet, but here is what we recommend:

Scoring Chart
Infantry..1,000 points
Sergeant..5,000 points
Lieutenant ....10,000 points
One-star general..............................21,000 points
Two-star general..............................22,000 points
Three-star general ....23,000 points
Four-star general ....24,000 points

Five-star general ....25,000 points
Information cards ....1,000 points
Unscrambled message ....15,000 points
Rules violations ....-10,000 points

Optional Rules

Number of generals. The number of generals you have on each team will depend upon the total number of players. Use two or three on each team if you have thirty players or less. But if you have thirty or forty per team, use a full five-star staff.

Promoting generals. If one general is captured, any surviving generals below that general's rank are automatically promoted one star. Simply note this on your list of personnel. No announcement is necessary.

Restoring lives. If you are playing the game with some sort of break in the middle (a dinner break is ideal in summer), it would be wise to evaluate the status of each team and very possibly restore lives. Always allow generals captured before the break to play as infantry after the break. While trying to steal information is a challenge, many scouts would probably prefer to return to the front as soldiers after the break. Restoring lives also tends to put the game back in the hands of a greater number of players as opposed to having the scouts and field marshals fight their somewhat isolated battles.

Survival bonus. When we have decided to restore lives, we have also given a survival bonus (we give 5,000 points) to any players who have reached the break without once being captured.

Capturing equals. We have discovered that when older and younger players play this game together, the older players can get too aggressive. The closer players are in age, the more fair they tend to be with one another. If your players comprise a wide range of ages, you may consider adding a rule that soldiers may capture only those of equal or higher rank (except the generals, who may still capture anyone).

Adults. If you have adults playing with your group, use them in the roles of field marshal and lieutenant. Designate two on each team as field marshals and the rest as lieutenants. Give the field marshals some type of identification tag that may be seen by any other player. You may also give the field marshals and lieutenants the option of changing roles at the break.

Extra Hints for Organizers

Here are some hints that may help your game of Outpost run more smoothly:

Playing site. One of the nice advantages of a vigorous chase game like Outpost is that you can play it almost anywhere that has significant cover. Of course, wooded areas provide better camouflage, but school campuses and neighborhoods can actually provide a better blend of hiding places and open areas. In any case, don't allow any indoor play. This can be risky as well as expensive.

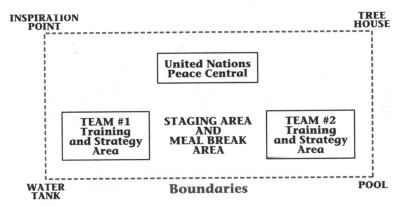

Generals. For years we played Outpost with only one general on each team. If your numbers are small, consider this option. It has both advantages and disadvantages. On the plus side, the capture of the general is a more significant event, an ultimate achievement. However, the risk of being captured is too great for many generals, and they often hide themselves (by burying themselves, climbing a tree, you name it) for the entire course of the game. When there are five generals, they are more willing to head out into the battle themselves, accepting the risk of being caught as fair trade for the active role of catching others.

Field marshals. The field marshal's role as tactician is not as instrumental in the basic version of Outpost as it is in the advanced version. In both games the field marshals are the strategists for their teams, but in the basic game it is more difficult for the field marshals to make quick contact with any teammates. Still, the field marshals should be able to direct the other players according to any knowledge about battle developments that they received during the course of the game.

Clothing. Inform your players beforehand that they must wear pants with back pockets if you are not using football flags.

UNPC. As Outpost organizers, we have taken particular pride in our United Nations Peace Central. We have used a large outdoor deck and decorated the railings with flags and other colorful banners. We have had as few as one organizer collecting information during the game, and as many as three. Once we even set up an old manual typewriter and typed out play-by-play action as it was reported from the front. This was quite a bit of extra work, but the players really enjoyed reading through the notes after the game was completed.

Outpost: Outline of Rules

Scenario
Two teams of equal size are pitted against each other in game that mimics modern combat.

Playing Time
One to five hours or more.

Stuff You Need
football flags or cloth strips
list of players
forty index cards
four extra copies of the rules
a location to act as UNPC
chalkboard

Characters
All players are designated as one of the following ranks:

Rank	Lives	Points
General(s)	1	20,000
Lieutenants	2	10,000
Sergeants	3	5,000
Infantry	3	1,000
Scouts	0	0
Field marshals	(cannot be captured)	0

Object
Players may earn points in three ways:

1. They may capture the other team's general(s).

2. They may capture enemy players.

3. Scouts may tag the field marshal for information.

United Nations Peace Central
United Nations Peace Central (UNPC) is a centrally located spot where rules are given, quarrels are resolved, captured players are turned in, and points are distributed.

Flags

1. Each team has its own colored flags.

2. Flags are worn by everyone in their back pockets. The flags must be able to be pulled freely from the pocket. At least one half of the flag must be hanging outside of the pocket to be visible.

Capturing the Enemy

1. Soldiers are captured and become prisoners when their flag is pulled from their pocket by an enemy.

2. Physical force may not be used in trying to pull a flag.

3. Players may not hold, sit on, or lean against anything when trying to defend their flags.

4. Once a capture has been made:

*All action stops for both players.

*Neither player may capture or be captured.

*The prisoner is escorted by the capturing player to the UNPC for points, or the capturing player may elect to set the prisoner free. All prisoners must be escorted by the capturing player, with one exception—generals may give captured prisoners to other players to be escorted back.

5. Field marshals cannot be captured.

Lives

1. All soldiers start with a designated number of lives according to their rank.

2. A life is taken away every time a soldier is captured.

3. When players run out of lives, they become scouts.

Scouts

1. Scouts can neither capture nor be captured.

2. Scouts play an important role in obtaining enemy information and locations.

3. Scouts may tag field marshals for information cards. These are turned in at UNPC for 1,000 points each.

4. Only scouts may try to unscramble the secret message formed by the information cards. The first team to figure out the secret message receives 15,000 points.

5. There are NO time-outs!

Ending the Game

The game ends when the organizers decide to end it, or when all of one team's generals have been captured. Scoring is figured according to the scoring table.

CHAPTER SIX

The Advanced Version
Outpost

AFTER NEARLY A DECADE OF PLAYING BASIC OUTPOST, we decided to buy one set of walkie-talkies for each team. This was not an overwhelming acquisition, but it prompted us to do a lot of creative thinking about how we could use walkie-talkies in our game, which is how we came up with an advanced version of Outpost. It can be played with as few sets as one per team, or with as many sets as you have available.

The walkie-talkies we purchased were the headset type, similar to those you see in many fast-food drive-throughs these days. Both of our sets were on the same frequency, which added to the suspense of the game because the teams automatically picked up each other's transmissions. The teams were forced to use code names and code words to keep their plans secret from one another. Your walkie-talkies may not be restricted to the same frequency, which challenges the teams to discover one another's channel. Either way it's fun for the teams to develop codes for their transmissions.

Much of the basic game of Outpost is retained in the advanced version. Kids and leaders who have played the basic version will easily make the transition to the advanced game, but those who haven't will pick it up just as easily.

Information cards are not used in the advanced version of Outpost. Instead of stealing information cards, the players get to bomb the command posts!

You will need to add one role to the advanced version that the basic version does not have—the role of communications specialist. The communications specialist may be a player of any rank. His role is to supply battle information, via walkie-talkie, to the army's command post. You will need one communications specialist for every walkie-talkie you have (except for the one used in the command post by the field marshal).

Stuff You Need

Besides walkie-talkies, the following extra materials are needed when playing Advanced Outpost:

Two tarps, eight to ten feet square. You may secure these tarps to trees or poles. The tarps will serve as cover for the command posts.

Ropes (and poles, if necessary). These are used to suspend the tarp above ground for the command post.

Large maps of the playing area. In most cases you will draw these yourself. They do not need to be precise but should at least show major landmarks, both natural and man-made. The field marshals will use the maps to plot strategy. The communications specialists may carry smaller versions of these maps. If the maps have grid references, they are especially helpful in relaying troop positions.

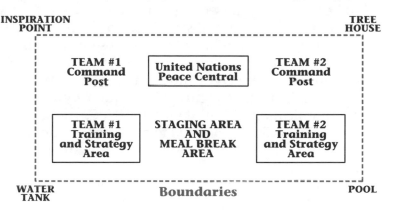

Container with sixty bomb cards in it. Twenty-four cards are labeled with a "B," twelve cards are labeled with an "O," twelve cards are labeled with an "M," and twelve cards are labeled "DEFUSE."

Ten old tennis balls. These are used as bombs. Number these balls from one to ten with a heavy black marker.

Two pieces of cardboard about 4 by 6 inches. These should have the word "RUNNER" boldly written on both sides. Give one card to each field commander to take to the command posts.

Chairs and tables (optional). If your field marshals are willing to haul these to their command posts, they will add to the atmosphere. It feels like a real war when field marshals sit in the battle zone writing out their plans.

Story and the Rules

When telling the basic Outpost story (Chapter Five), be sure to delete the rules about the information cards. You may weave the following rules into the basic story or simply add them at the end.

Each team will receive X number of walkie-talkies. One walkie-talkie is for the field marshal stationed at the command post. The rest will be given to soldiers. Soldiers carrying walkie-talkies are specially designated as communication specialists. These communication specialists have as many lives as their rank allows, but they lose their walkie-talkies the first time they are captured. Only scouts can capture the communication specialists, but the specialists themselves may capture as many soldiers as they wish. If a communication specialist is tagged by a scout, the scout escorts the communication specialist back to UNPC. The specialist does not lose a life, but the walkie-talkie is forfeited to the scout. Communications specialists who are forced to forfeit their walkie-talkies may then be captured by other soldiers and lose lives. Because scouts no longer have lives, they must immediately give any walkie-talkies they capture to another player with remaining lives. They can do this on the field or at the command post. If scouts are found with a walkie-talkie in their possession, they will be directed to go back to their command post and may be followed by the opposing army on the way.

Each army will be given a tarp as a command post. This command post should be set up in a spot known to your army, but well hidden from the opposition. The tarp should be suspended no higher than ten feet above ground. The command post cannot be moved at any time during the game. Field marshals will plot strategy within the boundaries of their command post. Besides field marshals, one player at a time is granted safety inside the command post. No soldier from one army may enter the command post of the other army. One walkie-talkie must always remain in the command post. *This last rule applies no matter how many walkie-talkies are being used.*

It is possible for one team to capture the other team's command post by bombing it. After a soldier becomes a scout, the soldier will draw a bomb card from a box at UNPC. This bomb card will have either a "B,"an "O," or an "M" written on it. It is also possible for a scout to be given a card marked "DEFUSE." All of these cards should be returned to the team's command post or other arranged meeting place. A scout cannot lose a bomb card to the other team. Once a team has acquired four cards spelling "BOMB," a scout may turn in the cards to UNPC for a live bomb (tennis ball). That team may then proceed to bomb the opponent's command post. *Organizers should distribute the bombs in numerical order and should record which team gets which bomb.*

In order to capture the opponent's command post, a scout must carry the bomb unnoticed to within throwing range of the command post. Before throwing the bomb, the scout must shout, "Bomb's Away!" If the bomb hits the top of the tarp, the command post is captured unless the field marshal can present a defuse card to the scout. This renders the bomb a dud. The field marshal then gives the defused bomb, the defuse card, and a runner card to a player. That player must return all three items to UNPC, where the bomb and bomb card are placed out of commission. Any player carrying a runner card to UNPC can neither capture nor be captured. After the bomb has been turned in, the runner should return the runner card to the command post.

Here are some other things to keep in mind when bombing a command post. First, if a scout throws a bomb and it misses the command post, it is considered live ammunition. It may be picked up only by the scout who threw it or by an opposing player with a defuse card. If the attacking scout recovers the bomb, it may be thrown again. If the bomb is picked up by a player with a defuse card, the bomb is a dud and it is returned to UNPC with the defuse card and a runner card by a runner. As before, the runner gets free passage to UNPC and the three items he carries are taken out of commission.

Second, it is possible to steal a bomb and use it for your team. Any scout carrying a bomb may be tagged by an opposing scout with a defuse card. The bomb is then defused and the scout must give up the bomb. The scout who has stolen the bomb must take it directly to UNPC. Passage to UNPC is not free because this player is not a runner. The bomb may be stolen again by an opposing scout with a defuse card.

At UNPC the defuse card is turned in and the bomb is re-registered to the new team. Remember that neither team can successfully bomb the opponent's command post unless the bomb is registered to the attacking team!

Third, a team may collect as many bombs as it wishes before making an attempt on the opposition's command post, but a scout can only carry one bomb at a time.

If one team successfully bombs the other's command post, the captured side must forfeit the walkie-talkie that is kept in the post. The bombing side receives 20,000 points. The captured side no longer has a hidden, protected place to meet. The field marshal who was manning the post must return to UNPC, from where he must direct the team for the rest of the game.

The End and the Score

Advanced Outpost finishes in the same way the basic version does. The game may end either when all five generals from one team have been captured or when the organizer decides it is time for a cease-fire.

Although Advanced Outpost is scored in much the same way as basic Outpost, we provide a complete score list for you here. Remember to make adjustments to these if you need the scoring to fit into some overall competition.

Scoring Chart

Infantry	1,000 points
Sergeant	5,000 points
Lieutenant	20,000 points
One-star general	21,000 points
Two-star general	22,000 points
Three-star general	23,000 points
Four-star general	24,000 points
Five-star general	25,000 points
Bombed command post	20,000 points
Promotion bonus	5,000 points
Rules violation	-10,000 points

Extra Hints for Organizers

In Advanced Outpost, we have found it best to have the lieutenants trade places with the field marshals at the break. This allows the field marshals to see some front line action, and it gives the lieutenants a breather.

It's great to have a walkie-talkie at UNPC. That way you can have a better grasp on what's taking place in the trenches. Hearing how the game is going will help you to determine when it might be best to call a cease-fire .

You have probably figured out by now that the game may be expanded or narrowed down simply by adding or taking away scoring objectives. The more people you have playing the game, the more players of high rank may be assigned. And if you have a huge number of people playing the advanced version, give each team more than one command post. One of the best things about Outpost is its versatility. You can arrange the teams and expand the game according to your needs.

Advanced Outpost: Outline of Rules

To play Advanced Outpost, use the rules for Outpost along with the following changes.

Stuff You Need
walkie-talkies (at least two sets)
rope
ten tennis balls
two torps
two cards marked "RUNNER"
bomb cards (according to the distribution defined)
map of playing area

Information Cards
Omit all rules concerning information cards. They are not used in Advanced Outpost.

Command Posts

A command post is a hidden strategy center in each team's territory. It should have some sort of cover overhead (such as a tarp) about eight to ten feet off the ground. Remember these important rules about the command post:

1. Field marshals direct their team's strategies from the command post during the game.

2. The command post cannot be moved during the game.

3. Only the field marshals and one other player may be inside the command post at any one time. The player inside the command post is immune from capture.

4. The command post may be bombed by the opposition.

Bombing

1. To prepare for bombing, teams must collect bomb cards.
*Bomb cards are kept at UNPC.
*When soldiers become scouts, they receive one bomb card at UNPC.
*Cards are marked with either a "B," "O," "M," or "DEFUSE."

2. To bomb the enemy command post, teams must follow this procedure:
*First, the team must acquire four cards that spell out the word "BOMB." A scout should then return the cards to UNPC to trade them for a live bomb (tennis ball).
*Each bomb is numbered so that the organizer can keep track of them after they have been distributed.
*Only scouts may use live bombs.
*The scouts try to throw a live bomb on top of the enemy command post. The scout must yell "Bomb's Away" when he throws the bomb.
*If the bomb hits the top of the enemy command post, the post is considered to be bombed unless the field marshal has a defuse card. If this is the case, the defuse card renders the bomb a dud. No damage is suffered.

*If the command post is successfully bombed, the field marshals must forfeit their walkie-talkies and return to UNPC for the rest of the game. The bombing team receives 20,000 points.

*If the bomb misses the top of the command post, it is considered live ammunition and may be picked up by the bomber or a player with a defuse card.

*If a bomb is defused, the bomb, the defuse card, and a card saying "RUNNER" are given to a player to return to UNPC. The bomb is out of play for the rest of the game.

*Runners may not be captured or capture other players during the time they are designated as runners.

3. Bombs may be stolen while they are being carried live by scouts.

*Scouts with defuse cards may tag scouts with live bombs to steal the bombs. Stolen bombs are then taken to UNPC to be re-registered by number to the new team.

Walkie-talkies

1. Use at least one set for each team.

2. One walkie-talkie must remain inside the command post.

3. Other walkie-talkies may be used only by soldiers with lives left. These soldiers are designated "Communications Specialists."

Communications Specialists

1. Communications specialists may be any soldiers with lives left.

2. These players keep the number of lives they have when assuming this rank. No extras are given.

3. There is one communications specialist for each walkie-talkie outside of the command post.

4. Communications specialists may be captured by scouts only, but the specialists may capture anyone.

5. If communications specialists are captured, their walkie-talkie is lost to the other team. They may then be captured by all other players.

Ending the Game

The game may end when the organizers choose or when all generals from one team have been captured. Scoring is figured according to the scoring chart for Advanced Outpost.

CHAPTER SEVEN

Ambush

THERE'S NOTHING MORE FUN THAN RUNNING through the woods like a wild Indian! Ambush is a game that combines the skilled tracking methods of the native Americans with an element of surprise. Ambush begins as a chase game, and then as it develops it adopts elements of both capture and hunt games.

In Ambush two Indian tribes battle each other for territorial rights. While tracking and ambushing one another in the wilderness, the Indians also try to capture the enemy village and obtain maps to the ancient burial grounds. Each action in the game depends on the one preceding it, but the surprise ambush controls all of the action.

Ambush requires larger groups than our other games; at least fifty players should be involved. It's more fun to play Ambush in a wooded area, although this is not absolutely essential.

Teams and Players

Ambush matches two Indian tribes against each other. Each tribe may have players who are both young and old, swift and slow, and sneaky and clumsy. Ambush is structured so that players are always actively able to pursue their opponents, no matter how strong or weak the players may be. Simply divide the total number of players in half, distributing the players evenly according to apparent ability. You also need to have some way of identifying the members of each tribe. The Extra Hints for Organizers section of this chapter gives ideas for simple and easy costumes that also identify each tribe.

Two organizers should act as tribal chiefs for the game. These organizers must remain impartial when interpreting the rules, but they may be strategy leaders for their respective tribes.

Stuff You Need

Two totem poles. These should be pieces of wood at least eight feet high. They may be logs, planks, or beams, and they should be easy to paint with regular tempera paints. The players should paint the poles well before the game is scheduled to be played (a day ahead is great). Painting the poles in advance gets the players caught up in the game before they even know the rules.

Two indelible markers. These are used by the tribal chiefs to distribute weapons and to keep track of the strength of the poles. Black or blue pens work best, and they must be have permanent ink that will not come off with water or sweat.

Two bottles of paint thinner and rags. The thinner is used to remove weapon markings from an Indian's hand. This is done when an Indian who has lost all of his strength chooses to change weapons. You should also have two rags to go with these bottles of thinner.

A large number of cut-up playing cards. These are used as strength tokens. Cut old cards into quarters. To be on the safe side, have twenty times as many cards as there are players. Each organizer should take half of these cards. (You may actually use any small token, but it is difficult to find anything as cheap, pocketable, and durable as plastic-coated playing cards. If you cut up six old decks, you will have enough cards for sixty players.)

Tempera paint. Indians will use this paint to decorate their totem poles.

Two balls of string. These are used to encircle the Indian totem poles about ten yards out on all sides. This circle forms the Indian village.

A diagram of the weapons arrangement. Draw the diagram on a chalkboard for the Indians to see while the rules are being given. The diagram should look like this:

Clues to the burial ground site. You will need one set for each Indian tribe. See Extra Hints for

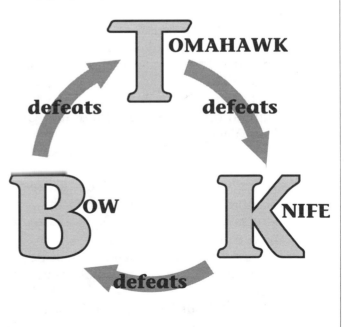

Organizers for an example of a clue list.

Treasure. Your treasure should not be so small that it could be hidden in an Indian's clothing, but it should not be so large that it requires more than one person to carry it. We have usually used simple, bulky items, such as a bag containing two old tents. The treasure does not need to be elaborate. After all this is burial property, not pirates' loot!

Story and Rules

Two chiefs enter the meeting of the Indians. One will give the rules while the other dances around the front of the room, chanting in a hushed voice and emphasizing the last words of important sentences by repeating them in the chant. The atmosphere is a blend of sobriety and humor. The chief telling the rules should be the straight man, while the dancing chief will provide the laughs. The chiefs should be appropriately dressed in headdresses, war paint, and beads.

"Good day of the sun, warriors! It has been many moons since our warpath has been walked on by Indian moccasins. I am Chief Fiery Spit, leader of Yosemite tribe. [Use whatever team names you have invented here.] My tribe has been challenged by Chief Spitfire and his Sierra tribe. We have come to this place of meeting atop Quintuk Mountain to set rules for war in Great Valley.

"To begin battle each warrior will be given one of three weapons: tomahawk, knife, or bow-and-arrow. It is important you know which weapon stronger. Tomahawk defeats knife, knife defeats bow, and bow defeats tomahawk. [Be sure to refer to the large chart you have made to show the players this arrangement. It is a also a good idea for you to have them repeat the arrangement after you.]

"The three weapons will be evenly distributed at beginning of war. One-third of you have tomahawks, one-third of you have knives, and one-third of you have bows.

"Your weapon will be written on palm of your right hand. T stand for tomahawk, K stand for knife, and B stand for bow-and-arrow. During battle, identify weapon to your opponent by raising right arm and showing him palm of hand. You try keep your hand closed and your palm hidden from opponent's sight until you forced to show it."

Be sure to give these examples and stop here to answer questions. Working out transactions is really very simple if all the players understand how they are made. If you explain the rules well, even young kids will have no difficulty with them.

"If you ambush another Indian and both of you have same weapon, stronger Indian always takes two tokens. No matter what difference in strength is, stronger Indian always takes two tokens. If strength is same, both Indians go their own way.

"You no allowed to ambush same Indian twice in row. But powerful Indian can be wiped out by group ambush. If two Indians with tomahawk ambush Indian with knife, tomahawks may trade off tagging knife until lone Indian has no more strength. To defend yourself to utmost, be sure not travel alone. Try to travel with people who have weapons different from your own. Beware group ambush!

"What should you do if strength is wiped out and you no tokens have? This very wise question from very weak warrior. Each team has own Indian village at site of its totem pole. At beginning of battle, each tribe set out to its Indian village. A circle of string around totem pole marks boundary of village. I will be at Yosemite totem pole and Chief Spitfire will be at Sierra totem pole. We are stationed at poles, but cannot guard Indian villages.

"If your strength as warrior is gone, go to village to receive new strength token. At this time, you may change weapon. You may select new weapon only if your strength completely wiped out. We will use Indian fire water to remove weapon from your hand, and we will inscribe new weapon on your palm.

"The totem pole is of great importance. Each totem pole represents strength of village. Villages begin with strength of 500. Any time pole is touched by Indian from other tribe, village's strength is decreased by strength of Indian. For example, if pole has strength of 500 and Indian with strength of thirty touches pole, strength of village decreases to 470. Same Indian cannot tag pole twice in row, and any Indian who tags pole must leave village boundary before tagging pole again. Only two Indians at time may enter village to touch pole. Any warrior touching opposing totem pole is free and has free walk out of village.

"Only one Indian at time can guard totem pole inside village, and warrior must have strength of twenty-five. This strong warrior is called tribal elder, and when he is inside village, Indian cannot lose, no matter what weapons are involved. An elder takes ten tokens from any Indian he tags inside village. These tokens are given to chief in village. They do not become property of elder. Outside village, elder is vulnerable to weapons. Remember, chiefs not guarding pole. Only elder may guard pole and only one elder in village at time.

"If you wish to give strength tokens to another player, you may. But you are forbidden to pass strength tokens across boundary of village. In other words, you may not give extra tokens to elder inside village. You may only give your strength tokens to elder if elder steps completely outside boundary of village.

"Now for ancient Indian secret. If you reduce strength of opponent's totem pole to zero, you will get set of clues that help you find Indian burial ground. This is where ancient treasure of tribe is buried. This list of clues will be given you by me or Chief Spitfire. There are two different burial grounds, one for each tribe.

"Once you have received clues, you go search for burial ground and treasure. When you find treasure, you must sneak treasure back and give it to tribal chief. If you are ambushed while you carry treasure and lose all strength, you must give treasure to Indian who ambushed you. You cannot steal treasure back and Indian who stole it must give it to his chief for safekeeping until end of game."

Now tell your tribes the boundaries and the time frame for the game. After you have answered questions, send the tribes to their villages where they will receive their weapons. You may give out the weapons randomly or allow the players to choose, but be sure that one-third of the Indians get tomahawks, one-third get knives, and one-third get bows. Have a trustworthy Indian or neutral party stay behind and give the signal to start the game after about ten minutes.

The End and the Score

You can end the game either when you run out of time to play or when one of the ancient burial treasures is found and returned to a tribe's village. We have played for a long time even after the treasure has been found. In either case you will need some sort of signal to inform players that the game is over.

Scoring for Ambush is simple. There are only a few things for which points are given. Use our chart if this is an exclusive event for you, or adjust the points as necessary to properly fit into your own overall point structure.

Scoring Chart
100 points for each strength token
25 points for each point lost from the totem pole
10,000 bonus points for wiping out the village
20,000 points for successfully turning in the opposing
tribe's burial ground treasure

You may also establish a bonus for Indians who end the game with a certain number of tokens. For instance you could give as much as 10,000 bonus points to any Indians who turn in more than fifty strength tokens.

Extra Hints for Organizers

Costumes. As you might imagine, Ambush really comes alive when the players wear costumes and war paint (regular tempera paint works well). Each team can invent its own war paint design to identify its braves. These markings, and any other costuming, should be done before the rules meeting so the Indians know the opponent's marking. This marking is just like a uniform and cannot be altered during the course of the game.

If you don't use war paint, you may want to try using headbands for one tribe and beads for the other. Whatever you choose to do, make sure you devise some way to tell the tribes apart.

Give strategy. Ambush is a game of strategy. The organizers, acting as chiefs, should give strategy tips to Indians as they return for new strength tokens and weapons.

*When giving strategy there is one ground rule—the chiefs cannot identify the strength of specific individual opponents to Indians of their own team. Beyond this there is no information that a chief cannot give his own tribe.

*Determining which weapons should be given to Indians who come back to the totem pole to have their weapons changed is an important piece of strategy. If the opponent's strongest Indians are carrying tomahawks, it might be best to give all returning Indians bows-and-arrows. If most of the opposing Indians tagging the pole seem to have knives, it would be wise to give your tribe tomahawks.

*Chiefs should also remind players to travel with braves who have different weapons than they do. Although confrontations are always one-to-one battles, other Indians can join in the confrontation. These Indians can in turn deplete a lone Indian's strength to zero. When Indians travel together though, they can protect one another with their weapons.

*Chiefs may also advise their Indians on how many braves should protect the village. Although the pole can only be guarded within the village by one tribal elder, it can be protected by other Indians who are outside the twenty-yard boundary of the village. It may not always be advantageous to protect the pole, however, especially early in the game when Indians are out trying to gather their own strength.

Ancient burial grounds. Creating the ancient burial grounds is easy. There should be one burial ground for each tribe. Actually, this is not a graveyard, so you do not need to make any real grave markings. You simply need to bury some sort of treasure in a rather specific place.

Designing clues. In designing clues to the burial grounds, use a written description as opposed to a map or riddle. Here is an example:

Yosemite Indian Treasure

1. Campfire.

2. 13 steps toward spiked tree, stand on knoll in rock.

3. Go 90 degrees left, 21 steps.

4. Follow pipe to white plastic.

5. Go 90 degrees right, 20 feet.

6. Look left to tallest tree, go to tree.

7. Go to opposite side of tree, look up.

8. Follow wire carefully to tree on Indian footpath.

9. Go to nearest plastic on ground.

10. Go to small pine tree in overgrown grassy area.

11. Look for large mound of dirt.

12. Stand on mound, sight small cut tree fallen between branches of another tree.

13. Follow ditch at base of tree to small granite rock.

14. Look to tallest of three skinny trees and go to that tree.

15. Look 90 degrees right to dead fallen tree.

16. Go to nearest end, dig.

Preparation time. It is important that you give yourself plenty of time to bury the treasures and chart the directions. If possible the organizers should each design one of the sets of clues and then work through the other's directions. This way you can work out any major problems in the two sets of clues. The two sets of clues should be similar in terms of the number of directions and the approximate territory covered to get to the treasure. (For more information on treasure hunts and clues, see Chapter Ten.)

Involve players. Ambush itself is an easy game but much of its success rests in its realism. Allow the tribes to be involved in the setup of the game as much as possible. Can they paint their own totem poles? Then have them do it! Can they create their own costumes? Then have them do it! Can they design their own war paint pattern? Then have them do it! Your players will so much more enjoy the actual game if they have had a strong hand in becoming true Indians just for this battle.

Ambush: Outline of Rules

Scenario
Two Indian tribes battle for territorial rights.

Playing Time
One to three hours.

Stuff You Need
two indelible markers
two balls of string
paint thinner and rags
one chalkboard
two logs to be used as totem poles
playing cards cut in quarters
tempera paint

Characters
Two organizers act as chiefs for each team. The chiefs interpret rules and

arrange strategies.
All other players are Indian braves.

Object

Players try to:

1. Ambush opponents and defeat them in battle to build up their strength.

2. Tag the enemy totem pole to decrease its strength.

3. Find the ancient burial grounds and the treasure buried there.

Ambushing Opponents

1. Three weapons are used: knife, bow-and-arrow, and tomahawk.
*One-third of your team will carry each weapon. Each player's
weapon is designated by writing a "K," "B," or "T" on the palm of his right hand in permanent ink.
*When in combat, the knife defeats the bow, the bow defeats the tomahawk, and the tomahawk defeats the knife.

2. Players carry tokens to indicate their strength. The more tokens, the greater the strength.

3. All players start with one token.

4. When one brave tags another, the two have entered into combat. Combat is always one-on-one.

5. Players declare their respective strengths first, then show their weapons.

6. Weapons determine the outcome of the combat.

7. If the weapons are the same, the stronger brave takes two tokens. If the two also have the same strength, nothing happens and both players go their own way.

8. If weapons are different, the players:
*Determine whose weapon prevails.

*The winner takes as many strength tokens from the loser as the winner currently has. If the loser has less tokens, the winner takes them all.

9. You cannot lose to the same person twice in a row. However, other enemy braves may tag you as soon as your first round of combat is resolved.

10. If you lose all of your strength tokens, return to the chief of your village. You will receive another token.

Villages and Totem Poles

1. Villages are an imaginary or roped off circle around the totem pole twenty yards in diameter. Chiefs stay within the village.

2. Totem poles are festively painted poles or boards put in the middle of the village. They are hidden in the woods from the opposing team, but placed in a fairly open area. The poles have a strength of 500.

3. If a pole is touched by an enemy player, its strength is decreased by the amount of strength of the warrior who has touched it.

4. Chiefs should keep a paper and pencil handy and visible.

5. Braves who touch the pole receive a free walk back outside the village. They may then attempt to touch the pole again. Only two braves may enter the village at one time.

6. Only players who have a strength of twenty-five or more may guard the pole.

7. Players tagged inside the village lose ten strength tokens. These are returned to the chief.

8. Guards inside the circle do not lose strength.

9. The chief is not a guard.

Ancient Burial Grounds

1. Directions to the ancient burial grounds are buried under the totem pole.

2. When the totem pole is reduced to zero strength, it is lifted out of the

ground and the directions to the ancient burial grounds are given to the conquering team.

3. The treasures of the tribe are located at the burial grounds.

4. Each team has a different burial ground. These need to be set up beforehand.

5. After the treasure is found, it must still be returned safely to the other village. If a brave is ambushed while carrying the treasure, the brave loses all strength and must give up the treasure, which is lost for the rest of the game.

Changing Weapons
Any braves who have zero strength may have their weapon changed by the chief. Use paint thinner to remove the old weapon, and mark the new one on the same palm.

Ending the Game
The game ends when the treasures have been found or the allotted time runs out.

CHAPTER EIGHT

Rockets' Red Glare

THERE IS NO AMERICAN HOLIDAY that is more steeped in history and tradition than the Fourth of July, and Rockets' Red Glare is the perfect Fourth of July game! The scenario for Rockets' Red Glare is based on the story of a last-ditch effort by the British redcoats to squelch the revolutionary effort. The British steal the new American flag and the

Liberty Bell and colonists must rise up once more and retrieve these important symbols of their new-found freedom.

Teams and Players

Rockets' Red Glare is played by two teams against the group leaders. It is best played in the half hour that is dusk, just before nightfall. The players on the two teams all belong to the revolutionary effort. They are led by the game organizers, who play the characters of Jacob McIntyre and his helpers, Gabriel and Jonathan.

The group leaders play the British redcoats who have stolen the Liberty Bell and the new American flag. Keep the amount of players to a maximum of fifty and have one redcoat for every six players (you need at least four redcoats, though).

Stuff You Need

Two regular highway flares. These are used to help the revolutionaries find the first checkpoint in their search for the flag or the bell. They need to be lit just before the players come out of their rules meeting, and they should be visible from the meeting room.

Buckets of water. These are used to safely extinguish the flares after the players have moved on to the second checkpoint.

Socks filled with flour. You need one of these for each redcoat. They are used as muskets. When colonists are struck with a sock, it will leave a white mark on their clothing. The socks should be filled about halfway with flour and then tied at the top. Athletic tube socks work best.

Coins or small tokens. These are given out by the redcoats when they are bound by four revolutionaries. They are worth extra points at the end of the game.

Cups to collect the coins. At the end of the game, you need two cups (one for each team) to collect the coins that are brought in by the players.

American flag. You need one standard-sized American flag. An older flag that has fewer stars than our current one works especially well. The flag is one of the items that has been stolen by the redcoats.

"Liberty" bell (or some substitute). A good-sized bell with a crack painted in it makes a perfect Liberty Bell. If you can't get a bell, find a good substitute: a crate of tea, Paul Revere's lanterns, or a copy of the Declaration of Independence.

Clothes brush. This will be used to remove the flour that represents musket wounds.

Electronic flash units (optional). Flash units of cameras can add to the mood by looking like shell fire in the distance.

Story and Rules

Several characters tell the Rockets' Red Glare story. Any group organizers who are good at acting can play a part. The fellow who tells the story is Jacob McIntyre. He comes in wearing tattered clothes and walking slowly, as if in pain. There's a wound on his side from one of the flour sock muskets. His two partners (who also serve as team leaders)—Gabriel and Jonathan—are in better shape and help Jacob along.

Jacob may give the rules in two ways. If you are at a camp where your group can change clothes in a hurry, he should enter at the end of your evening meeting and tell the first part of his story. You can then send the players to change into dark clothes and instruct them to return to hear the rest of the rules. If you are not in a place where clothes can be changed easily, you will need to tell your players before they show up for the game to wear dark clothes. If this case, Jacob can tell the rules in one sitting.

When Jacob enters, the room should be dark. The group may be noisy at first. After all they are revolutionaries. In a moment, however, they will realize that they must be quiet, because Jacob McIntyre is extremely weak and cannot talk in a loud voice. As he tells his story, the injured Jacob seems to weave in and out of full consciousness.

"They have stolen the Liberty Bell! They have stolen the Stars and Stripes! If they make off with these symbols of our freedom, the revolution will be severely hindered. We cannot let those mangy redcoats get away with this. We must fight back! We have worked too hard and come too far to let them take these things away from us now!"

The next paragraph should only be used by those who have the ability to send their group back to change.

"Go now! Return to your homes and put on dark clothes. We must use the cover of dusk if we are going to recover our stolen items. We need all of your help to keep the revolution alive. The king shall not defeat us, and neither shall his army! Remember, wear dark clothes. You will need them to move safely in the night. Return as soon as you can."

When the players return, you may continue. If you have not sent your players to change, resume the story here.

"The redcoats have stolen two important symbols of our freedom. We must get them back. We are lucky—we have friends everywhere. Our friends have closely followed the band of soldiers who stole the bell and flag. We still have time to catch them and get these symbols of our revolutionary struggle back. The redcoats have always been poor soldiers. It will be easy for us to follow their trail.

"Still we must be careful. There are redcoat soldiers along the whole route carrying muskets. If you are shot with a musket, it will leave a powder wound similar to the one I have here on my side. The wounds are usually nothing to worry about. If you are wounded, come back here. I was a doctor before this war began, and I will quickly dress your wound for a small fee of points and send you back into action.

"Do not kill a redcoat. Instead you must bind him and try to get information. You bind a redcoat by grabbing his legs. Once you have grabbed his legs, he will think you are just an innocent child and he will not hurt you. Do not let go of the redcoat; others will soon be there to help you. When four of you have a redcoat by the legs, he will surrender to you. Each of you will receive a small coin from the redcoat. This is the pay he has recently received from the British government. Keep the coins. We will collect them for the war effort after the bell and flag have been recovered.

"After you have bound a redcoat, stay attached to him until all the other guards at the checkpoint are bound. When all the redcoats guarding a particular checkpoint have been bound, one of them will give you a clue to the next checkpoint. Figure out the clue, and then try to get to the checkpoint as soon as you can. Then bind the redcoats at this checkpoint. You will work through several checkpoints until you finally recover the bell or the flag.

"Because we must recover both the Liberty Bell and the flag, we need to split you into two squads. Is there a way to do that?"

If your kids are already divided into two teams, they will shout "Yes!" If not you can divide the teams in any way you like, although boys against girls would probably be easiest.

"All of you on this side will go with Gabriel. He will lead you out the front door."

It is best if you have two opposite exits from the same room. Then you can send out your players with little confusion.

"All of you on that side go with Jonathan. He will lead you out the front door.

"The first checkpoint will be seen at the Rockets' Red Glare."

You should then answer any questions. Because the game follows a set pattern, you don't have to worry about laying out boundaries. One of the first questions the kids will ask is, "How can I find the first checkpoint?"

Jacob should answer, "All I can tell you is that the first checkpoint will be seen at the Rockets' Red Glare."

After this Jacob faints and leaves the game temporarily until the first colonists return to have their wounds dressed.

Setting up the Checkpoints

As the organizer you need to determine and set up the checkpoints before the game. While this will require good organization and a little creativity, if you know your playing area fairly well, it shouldn't take more than a half hour. If you aren't too familiar with your playing field, it may take you as long as an hour. You will also need to meet for about a half hour with the leaders who will be your redcoats so you can explain to them how to protect the checkpoints and how to distribute the clues.

For each object (Liberty Bell, flag, etc.) you use—and you may use more than two if you have more people or more teams—you will need five or six checkpoints. After one checkpoint has been captured, the redcoats will turn over the clue leading to the next checkpoint. Remember that the first checkpoint does not have a clue because it is marked by the Rockets' Red Glare, which is the glow of the highway flare.

Here is an example of checkpoints and clues we have used:

1. Flare...(campfire circle)
2. "Where the water stops" ....(small dam)
3. Indian practice ground...............(archery range)
4. Little living place........................(smallest cabin)
5. Below mini men.....................(under boys' dorm)
6. Upside and outside............................(tree house)

Before the game you should divide your leaders into groups of redcoats. There should be one group of redcoats for each set of checkpoints. Each group should be made up of no fewer than two redcoats.

These redcoats will guard the various checkpoints. When the game begins, half of the redcoats in each group should be stationed at the first checkpoint, the highway flare. The other half should be at the second checkpoint. When the redcoats who are guarding the first checkpoint have all been bound and the clue to the next checkpoint has been given, the first redcoats should progress to the third checkpoint and prepare to guard it. In this way the redcoats play a sort of leapfrog, with half of each group guarding the even-numbered checkpoints and half of the group guarding the odd-numbered checkpoints. Here is a diagram that should help you understand this setup a little better:

It's best to write the clues and checkpoints on in-dex cards for each group of redcoats. Remember that the

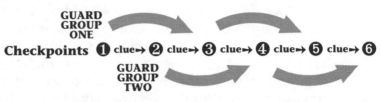

guards at the even-numbered checkpoints should have the clues to the odd-numbered checkpoints, and vice versa.

The End and the Score

Rockets' Red Glare ends very simply. When the bell and the flag have been found, the game is over. The players earn a bonus for each coin they turn in at the end of the game.

You should use the following scoring allotment if you don't need to fit the scoring into an overall point system. If you are using Rockets' Red Glare as part of an overall competition, you may need to modify the point structure.

Scoring Chart
First object returned (bell or flag) ......10,000 points
Second object returned.........................5,000 points
Each coin returned ....1,000 points
Each first aid given.................................-100 points

Extra Hints for Organizers

Because you are using highway flares, be sure that you use them in a fire-safe area. The redcoats at the first checkpoint should extinguish the flare with water immediately after the checkpoint has been captured.

For an ideal beginning, try to arrange the first checkpoints so one team cannot see the red glare of the other team's flare. One way to do this is to send the first team out a door on one side of the building, and the other team out a door on the other side of the building. If this isn't possible, be sure to show each team which flare it should be pursuing. Try to avoid having the teams cross paths. In the settling darkness of dusk, it is easy for players to get confused and pursue the wrong goals with the wrong people.

You may try to arrange to have more redcoat guards at the first checkpoint than at the others. At the beginning of the game, all of the players will be heading for the checkpoint together and the onslaught will be tough for the redcoats to handle. After a few of the players have been wounded and leave the game temporarily to receive first aid, the redcoats will have a better chance.

When you talk with the leaders who play the redcoats, be sure to let them know that they do not need to whip their sock muskets with tremendous force to make a mark. This is especially important if you are playing with younger kids. While the socks don't really hurt, they can surprise players who do not see them coming.

When players return to have their wounds dressed, you need only to brush the flour from their clothes. A clothes brush makes the job easier.

If you have more than fifty people playing the game, you'll need to set up more checkpoint paths. You don't want to have more than about twenty-five people going after the same object. Rockets' Red Glare can become confusing if players from different teams get mixed in with one another. If you use smaller groups, the players are less apt to split up and go off in odd directions.

Rockets' Red Glare can literally explode with thrilling atmosphere. The redcoats can add a realistic effect by carrying electronic flash units (like those you would use on a camera) and flashing these from time to time to give the effect of shell fire in the distance. And if you are actually able to play on the Fourth of July, it is unbelievably exciting to play near a fireworks show. The lights and booming sounds from the fireworks will make your game a holiday spectacular.

Rockets' Red Glare: Outline of Rules

Scenario
On July 4, 1776, British redcoats stole the Liberty Bell and the new American flag. The new American patriots must get them back!

Playing Time
Forty-five minutes at dusk.

Stuff You Need
two highway flares
cups to collect coins
buckets of water
American flag
flour-filled socks
bell
coins or small tokens

Characters
Leaders are the redcoats.
Players are the patriots.

Object
Players earn points by binding redcoat guards, getting their coins, and obtaining clues to the location of the bell or flag, which is the ultimate goal.

Binding Redcoats

1. To bind a redcoat, four patriots must successfully latch on to the legs of a redcoat by using their hands or arms.

2. Redcoats have muskets (flour-filled socks) that are used to wound the patriots.

*Redcoats can hit patriots with musket shot from any location, but they will mainly be at redcoat checkpoints.

*When shot, patriots must return to their home base immediately.

*Jacob, the game leader, will be at the home base to record the musket hit against the appropriate team and to give the patriots first aid.

*After being tagged by Jacob, patriots continue on to the redcoat checkpoints.

*When being bound, a redcoat may not hit that patriot with musket shot.

*If a patriot is attached to a redcoat's legs, no other redcoat can shoot that patriot.

*A redcoat may continue to shoot at "free" patriots (those not attached), as long as there are less than four patriots attached to the redcoat's legs.

3. When being bound, a redcoat cannot try to kick or pull off patriots.

4. Patriots attached to redcoats may not tackle, tickle, or hit.

5. Once bound by four patriots, a redcoat can no longer use his musket while at that checkpoint.

6. Any patriot trying to steal a redcoat musket will be removed from the game.

Stealing Redcoat Coins

1. Redcoats possess four gold coins for each checkpoint they protect.

2. When a redcoat is bound by four patriots, each patriot will get one gold coin.

3. Once a redcoat has been bound, the patriots must stay attached to that redcoat until all other redcoats are bound. A patriot may bind only one redcoat per checkpoint.

4. Patriots hold on to coins until the end of the game when they will be turned in for points.

Getting the Clues and Goal

1. When all the redcoat guards at a checkpoint are bound, the checkpoint is considered overtaken.

2. Patriots ask the guards where their goal (bell or flag) is. Redcoats give patriots a clue to the location of the next checkpoint.

3. Patriots continue to overtake checkpoints until the redcoats do not give a clue. Because no clue is given, the goal must be hidden nearby.

4. Patriots search around the checkpoint to find the hidden goal. When the goal is discovered, it must be taken back to home base.

Ending the Game
Rockets' Red Glare ends with a loud signal at the end of playing time or when the bell and flag have been captured. Everyone gathers, tells stories, and the leaders announce scores.

Over the Wall

OVER THE WALL BORROWS ITS SCENARIO from a significant event in history, the building of the Berlin Wall. Because the Berlin Wall was erected overnight, the decision to cross the wall while it was being built had to be made in a split second. Those who may have attempted to cross into freedom that first night had little time to think about the consequences, little time to pack their belongings, and little time to say goodbye to friends. Over the Wall is a night game that re-enacts what may have happened in the hours before the wall separated West Berlin from the rest of East Germany.

Players in Over the Wall attempt to get from East Berlin to West Berlin and vice versa. They must make the switch before the routes in and out of West Berlin are closed.

Teams and Players

Over the Wall pits two teams against one another and against a third, smaller group. We've been successful matching teams of boys against teams of girls. The third group has been made up of counselors, who play the guards along the wall. This group should be about one-sixth as large as the number of other players. So if you have fifty kids, you need about eight leaders to act as guards.

The organizer of Over the Wall can participate in the game as a guard if necessary.

Stuff You Need

Rope. You need enough rope to span the width of your playing area at least once. Two lengths of rope work even better. The rope represents the wall. The lengths do not need to be continuous (walls or trees may interrupt the line), but you will need to be able to have some way of tying the ropes taut about three or four feet above the ground.

Flashlights. There should be one flashlight for every two guards. The flashlights are used to spot would-be defectors.

Four large pieces of cloth. These are hung at the four corners of the playing field to mark the overall boundaries.

*A **bullhorn** (optional).* You can use a bullhorn to announce how much time is left during the course of the game to add an element of suspense and urgency.

*More **ropes.*** Ropes may be used to define the area of the holding cells (optional). These are laid on the ground to mark the boundaries of the holding cells. They need to be long enough to form circles ten to fifteen feet in diameter. You also might use a ring of ropes or other small items to mark the holding cells.

Playing Site

More than any of the other games in this book, Over the Wall requires a specific playing area. Below is a layout of the field.

The playing area should be approximately 200 yards long and 50 yards wide. The number of obstacles in the area is not important, but you need an area that is neither completely open nor

overwhelmed by large buildings. The boundaries must also be clearly marked by sheets or some other objects that are visible in the darkness.

Story and Rules

It is best to gather the players of Over the Wall in a tightly packed, dimly lit room. Give them the impression that they are in a very secret meeting. The players and the organizer should, if possible, wear dark clothes, but no other costumes are necessary. The storyteller should convey seriousness and urgency as he is giving the rules.

"It is August 13, 1961. The city is Berlin. Tonight, communist workers are erecting a high fence that will cut off the west half of the city. Without specific government permission, no man or woman will be permitted to enter or exit West Berlin. Tonight is your last chance to go in or out of West Berlin. To make the crossing, you must successfully get by the guards who are patrolling the wall without being captured."

At this point, be sure your players are aware of the boundaries of the playing field. Because the area is relatively small, the players need to know exactly where the landmarks are. You may even want to show them a large diagram of the playing field. It is also a good idea to mark the four corners of the playing area with some light-colored markers, such as big white flags.

"The boys [or however you have divided your group] will start at the boundary nearest to us; the girls will begin at the boundary at the far end. Boys, you are starting in East Berlin and are trying to get to West Berlin. Girls, you are starting in West Berlin and are trying to get to East Berlin. Your goal is to safely cross the wall and reach the other boundary on the other side. You will be not safe until you have reached the other boundary.

"Between you and your goal is the wall. At this time the wall is only two lines of rope about two and four feet above the ground. Do not try to run through the wall in the dark. You may be hurt and the guards will capture you. You may go over, under, or between the ropes.

"Half of the guards who are patrolling near the wall carry scanning lights that will allow them to spot you in the night. The lights themselves cannot hurt you, but if a guard tags you, you will be taken to a holding cell. The holding cells are located at either side of the wall. Do not resist the guards. If you cooperate you will almost certainly get another chance to cross the wall to reach your goal.

"Half of the guards are stationed on one side of the wall, and half have been stationed on the other side. They do not change sides. By government orders these guards are also directed to go no more than twenty yards away from the wall. As for their scanning lights, only one guard on each side has a scanning light that operates continuously. All of the other lights are weaker and may be turned on for only five seconds at a time, and then must be turned off for ten seconds. You must be as quiet as possible and hide behind trees and rocks when you are near the wall. When a light shines on you, do not panic. If you are near the wall, retreat quickly to an area outside the twenty-yard range before a guard tags you.

"If you get past the wall, you are still not totally safe. Any guard or citizen on the other side of the wall may tag you and escort you to the holding cell. If you make noise once you get past the guards, they may follow you with their scanning lights so that the citizens can find you and tag you. Be careful until you have reached your final goal. When you do reach the opposite boundary, wait there for others. The team that gets the most players to the other boundary by the end of the game is the winner.

"If you are taken to a holding cell, you must stay there until six prisoners have been captured by the guards or turned in by citizens. When six prisoners are in the cell, a guard will escort all six back to the beginning boundary. This guard may not capture anyone else while he is escorting the captives nor may he take any prisoners on the way back. Watch for guards escorting their captives back to the beginning boundary. When the guard is away from his post, you have a perfect opportunity to try and get through! If the guards wish, however, they may escort prisoners only to the twenty-yard boundary. The prisoners will not have as far to return to the wall, but the guards will not be away from their posts for very long.

"The holding cells may be circles of rope or just informal areas at the ends of the wall. The guards stationed at the ends of the wall can keep an eye on the prisoners in the holding cell, who usually tend to be cooperative and take advantage of their captivity to spy on the patterns of those who are guarding the wall.

"You will have only thirty minutes to reach your goal. Move quickly and quietly to avoid danger. Good luck."

The End and the Score

If there is a limit to the time that you have to play this game, then end it when you need to. Most games last about a half an hour. When the time for the game to end is near, start using your bullhorn frequently. Give the players warnings like this one:

"Attention! Attention! It is now 0445 hours. Any citizens attempting to pass the wall after 0500 hours will be subject to life imprisonment or immediate execution. You have fifteen minutes."

Scoring for Over the Wall is very basic. When the game is over, simply count the number of players on each team on the opposite side of the wall. Some players will undoubtedly tell you that they made it over three, four, even ten times, but laugh it off and tell them they probably snuck past the guard who was asleep. Each player gets counted only once.

Extra Hints for Organizers

The only tough part for the organizer of Over the Wall is getting the game set up. Make sure you create good, recognizable boundaries and that you create a realistic facsimile of the wall. It's best if your wall is not one unbroken line of rope. Rather, it should be randomly broken up by trees, small buildings, trash cans, or anything that will provide cover for the players and guards. You might want to use a double line of rope so that the players have a little more difficult time going under the wall. Make sure that the ropes are very taut, so that they cannot be pushed down and stepped over easily. You can hang cloth or old sheets over portions of the wall to make the game even more difficult. But be careful not to make it so tough that no one succeeds.

There is only one significant element of strategy in Over the Wall, and you might mention this strategy to the players before you begin. Because the teams do two things at once—reach their own goal and defend the opponent's goals, they need to decide just how soon they want to try to send all of their players over the wall. The teams may decide to hold back as many as half of their players for a while to serve as citizens who may capture members of the other team.

Over the Wall is probably the simplest game in this book. It is an excellent game for large groups who do not have a lot of space. It is also a great game to play before a movie is shown, particularly a movie like Night Crossing, which is about escaping over the wall from East Berlin to West Berlin. And organizers will love Over the Wall since they can join the game's action as participants rather than just observers.

Over the Wall: Outline of Rules

Scenario
Set during the overnight building of the Berlin Wall, Over the Wall challenges players to cross from one side of the wall to the other, while avoiding German guards.

Playing Time
Thirty to forty minutes at night.

Stuff You Need
bullhorn (optional)
one or two 150-foot lengths of rope
four large pieces of cloth
flashlights

Playing Area
The playing area should be laid out as shown at right.

Characters
Leaders are German guards.

Players are citizens of Berlin.

Object
East Berlin citizens try to cross the wall and get to the West. West Berlin citizens try to cross the wall and get to the East.

The Wall
The wall is set up by stringing one or two ropes taut across the width of the playing area.

Crossing the Wall
When trying to cross the wall, the citizens must sneak past the guards, who are holding flashlights and scanning the area.

1. Players begin at their boundary slowly moving toward the wall.

2. Guards protect the wall with their flashlights. Only half of the guards have flashlights. The flashlights are not weapons.

3. Guards may shine their lights for five seconds, then they must turn off the lights for a ten-second recharging period. One guard on each side of the wall has a flashlight that operates continuously.

4. The guards may not wander more than twenty yards from the wall.

5. If a player is tagged by a guard within the twenty-yard range, the player is taken to one of the holding cells at both ends of the wall. When six players are in the holding cell, they are all escorted back to their home boundary by one of the guards.

Getting Past the Other Side
Just because a player has safely crossed the wall does not mean that player is safe. The player must still get by the other citizens.

1. If a player is tagged by a citizen of the other side, that citizen takes the player to the holding cell. During this escort, both players are free from further capture.

2. Guards are allowed to shine their scanning lights on players entering the

opposite side, exposing them to the citizens for capture.

3. Citizens who escort a prisoner to the holding cell get a free passage back to their own city, beyond the twenty-yard guard zone. They may not cross the wall and attempt to enter the opposite side until they have first returned to their own city.

Ending the Game

The game's end should be led up to with announcements over the bullhorn. Thirty or forty minutes is usually plenty of time for this game. Over the Wall is won by the team that has the most players successfully reach the opposite boundary.

CHAPTER TEN

Designing a Masterful
Treasure Hunt

OFF THE COAST OF EASTERN CANADA there is a tiny island rumored to be the devil's northern lair. This island, a deep hole, known as the Money Pit, has claimed the lives of six hapless treasure seekers. Legend demands the death of a seventh before the hole will yield its secret. What's in the Money Pit? Some say it is Captain Kidd's booty. Others

119

suggest the crown jewels of some European country are hidden there. A small number of people even propose that Francis Bacon's manuscripts—the same manuscripts that would prove Bacon to be William Shakespeare—lie at the bottom of the hole.

There are thousands of stories like these that keep the lure of buried treasure alive in the minds of youngsters and adults alike. And like all fascinating and mysterious stories, legends of buried treasure provide fantastic opportunities for developing adventures. Treasure hunts can make up the entire adventure game itself or you can use a hunt as part of a larger adventure game (as we did in Ambush, Safari, and Bounty Run, for example). However you decide to use treasure hunts, you'll discover that they have two distinct advantages: the hunts can be geared in difficulty to the level of any group of players and they may be designed to fit almost any theme or story line.

How to Get Started

Designing a treasure hunt takes time. The bigger the hunt, the more planning time it generally takes. A good rule of thumb is that it will take about twice as long to set up a hunt as it will for the seekers to find the treasure.

Treasure hunts require props or tools. The kinds of props and tools needed depend on where the treasure is hidden and how the seekers are to find it. You will certainly want to include a treasure map of some kind, whether it is an actual map or contains clues or riddles, and you will need an object to act as the treasure. It doesn't need to be an exotic treasure; after a long and spirited hunt, most players just want to say they found the treasure, be it a watermelon, an old trophy cup, or a small marble egg.

Four Types of Treasure Hunts

Treasure hunts have many different themes and various levels of grandeur, but there are really only four basic types of treasure hunts—the riddle hunts, treasure paths, the clue-to-clue hunts, and map hunts. All four are equally demanding, and only one, the riddle hunt, requires less set-up time.

Riddle hunts.

The riddle hunt, made famous in Edgar Allen Poe's short story, "The Gold Bug," is a hunt in which players answer a riddle or a series of riddles to find their treasure. A riddle hunt can be extremely difficult for the players, but it is fairly easy for the organizers to set up.

The riddle itself needs to be a short set of lines, rhyming or non-rhyming, which gives the location of the treasure. The seekers must unlock the meaning of the riddle to find the treasure.

In Poe's "The Gold Bug," William LeGrand figures out the location of Captain Kidd's treasure by deciphering the following riddle:

A good glass in the bishop's hostel in the devil's seat forty-one degrees and thirteen minutes northeast and by north main branch seventh limb east side shoot the left eye of the death's head a beeline from the tree through the shot fifty feet out.

Obviously you need to read the story to find out how LeGrand works through this clue, but you can get the picture of what kind of riddle may be used to begin your hunt. Here is an example of a riddle we have used:

Along the walker's road
Lie some groups of boards
Count two, then three—now stop
And gather in the hoards.

As you might have deduced, the treasure was hidden under the third board ("count three") of the second bridge ("count two"…groups of boards) along a known trail ("the walker's road").

You'll need to keep a number of things in mind when you're setting up a riddle hunt. First, consider carefully the ages of your seekers. Use language and vocabulary that they can understand. The riddle can include puns or messages with double meanings as long as the riddle can be deciphered in the end. Second, the riddle should involve places that are familiar to the seeker, but at the same time not completely give away the hidden treasure's location. Don't identify a place that is completely unknown to your seekers. You must be especially aware of this if you are planning a treasure hunt for a site with which your players are unfamiliar.

The riddle hunt can be used as one of the elements of a bigger hunt or adventure game. To make a hunt more complicated, we sometimes split the riddle into two parts, both of which must be obtained to complete the riddle. Or we use a single riddle as one of many clues in a bigger hunt. (This works well in a game like Bounty Run, where a large number of clues are put together to find the treasure.)

Treasure paths.
Treasure paths use a type of word map to point to the treasure. Before the hunt the seekers are given an entire list of directions and they must follow each of the directions in the order given to find their treasure. This is an excellent kind of hunt for younger seekers because it teaches them to patiently and methodically work through directions.

Here's an example of a treasure hunt that has worked well for us:

The Great Yosemite Sierra Treasure Hunt
1. Begin at the large rock near the crafts tent.
2. Face west and spot tallest tree.
3. Go approximately halfway to tree.
4. Look under right rock for an item to help you.
5. Follow straight edge of sharp point of same rock to chopped-off tree.
6. Stand on stump, facing tree.

7. From current direction, face left. Spot sandy place.

8. Go to this place and dig for another item that will help you in your search.

9. Return to last stump.

10. Face right from original direction.

11. Spot bent tree and go to base of it.

12. Follow direction of bent tree to Y tree.

13. Sit in Y tree facing west—one leg on each side.

14. Look forty-five degrees left to huge stump in distance.

15. Go to stump, but stand on second stump you couldn't see from Y tree.

16. From the stump look for cement blocks with handles.

17. Go to these blocks and count the number of blocks whose handles you can see. Remember this number!

18. From the headlight of the Cushman cart, go straight to the lone pine in your vision.

19. There is a small holly bush under a manzanita along this line. Stop there.

20. Face the Pinnacles.

21. Turn a smidgen to the right and spot small, dead tree.

22. Walk toward that tree. Be careful—you will lose sight of the tree.

23. Stop at the rock on the pipe.

24. Follow pipe left until it disappears.

25. Go to skinny leafless tree forty-five degrees to the right.

26. Look right toward small door.

27. Spot submerged rock.

28. From the rock's left point, walk as many steps as there were cement blocks with handles.

There is your treasure!

In directions four and eight, there is reference to finding items that will help the seeker. The first item is a steak knife, and the second is a stack of paper plates. The treasure in this particular hunt is a watermelon, and the knife and paper plates will be used to prepare the final feast. By including items like these early in the hunt gives the seekers a feeling of success and the knowledge that they are on the right track. It also increases the suspense about what the treasure really is!

You'll also notice that direction thirteen involves the seeker in a specific action—sitting in a tree. By including directions in which the seeker actively participates in the hunt in some sort of physical way keeps the seekers involved and paying careful attention to the directions.

It's important to use landmarks like these in a treasure path to orient the seekers. Any landmarks should be permanent ones or at least stationary for the duration of the hunt. Direction eighteen refers to a headlight of a vehicle. The vehicle we used was an old utility cart that had seen its last days of action and certainly wasn't going anywhere for the time we needed it.

Because seekers on treasure paths have all their clues given to them at the beginning of a hunt, it is important to make sure that any directions given later in the clue list will not allow the seekers to skip any of the earlier ones. If a familiar place such as a tree house is identified, it should only be used as a landmark related to other places, not as a stopping point along your path. This way the familiar place is only important as it is linked to another place, a place unfamiliar to the seekers.

For another example of a treasure path, see the Extra Hints for Organizers in Chapter Seven, Ambush.

Clue-to-clue hunts.

A clue-to-clue hunt is a treasure hunt that leads its seekers through a series of clues. When one secret spot is found, a clue is given to the next secret spot. Clue-to-clue hunts are similar to treasure paths, except that the seekers do not receive an entire list of directions at the beginning of the hunt.

To prepare a clue-to-clue hunt, the organizer develops a treasure path on paper, and then leaves clues at each spot along the path. These clues may be riddles or simple directions just like those in a treasure path.

Clue-to-clue hunts have some real strengths. First, they allow the seekers to feel successful again and again. Each time the seekers find the next clue, they know they are on the right path. Second, these hunts are good for games like Bounty Run where one team is trying to stop another from getting to the treasure. The team doing the seeking can stop and start its search depending on how well it is being followed. Last, clue-to-clue hunts do not allow players to skip directions because the players get only one direction at a time.

But clue-to-clue hunts have one big disadvantage. They are difficult to play if two or more teams are competing to find the same treasure. If one team gets to a location first and takes the only clue, the trailing team is lost for a good portion of the game. This problem can be remedied by stationing people at various points to give out the clues. The seekers must identify themselves to the clue givers by giving a password. Only then will the clue givers relinquish their clues to the seekers. The clue givers need to have enough clues for each team playing the game.

A Wild Goose Chase is a fun-filled version of a clue-to-clue hunt that several Youth for Christ groups around the country have played with large groups. In a Wild Goose Chase the teams—traveling by cars, vans, and buses—are led through a chain of clues to various points in their city until one team finds a live goose and returns it to the starting point to claim victory. In order to find the clue givers, the teams have to repeat the phrase "Goosey, goosey gander, where do you wander?" to the right person. Repeating the phrase to the wrong person, usually a total stranger, can be embarrassing on both sides, but it makes the game a whole lot of fun!

Treasure map hunts.

Argh, this is one fer da pirates amongst ye! Treasure map hunts are great fun, but one important principle must be followed: the seekers need to be oriented to the locations on the treasure map. If you lived in Los Angeles and were given a treasure map of buried loot somewhere along the Mississippi, you would need to know what area the map covered to know where to begin. Game organizers must make sure to give the seekers some idea of where to start their search.

The treasure map should not include too many pictures. It should include written hints that will get the seekers to the place the map covers. The fewer landmarks shown on the map, the trickier the map hunt will be.

Give the maps an authentic touch. When we put on a hunt with a pirate theme, we use pirate dialect on the map. It also helps to draw the map on dirty parchment and burn the edges with a match. Roll up the map and tie it with a bit of twine. Below is an example of a map we used on a Pirates' Day a few years ago.

The Theme Makes it Great!

A treasure hunt really comes alive when it has a special theme or is tied to an event. Here are some ideas about a few possible themes.

Pirates. The pirate theme is the classic treasure theme. With some good research into lost pirate treasures (including a look at "The Money Pit" and "The Gold Bug"), you can add to the authenticity of your hunt.

Explorers. There are many great stories in history about explorers hunting for treasures. Ponce de Leon's search for the Fountain of Youth and Coronado's quest for the Seven Gold Cities both work as well starting points for treasure hunts.

Indians. In California the Indians were instrumental in helping the Spanish missionaries protect church valuables against the feisty bandits of the great Old West. Some of these valuables were so well hidden that they were never found again—either by their owners or by the bandits. Seekers can find these long-lost treasures in the fantasy adventure of a treasure hunt.

Gold mines. The California gold rush of 1849, the lost gold mines of Nevada, and the Outlaw Trail of Colorado and Utah provide outstanding backdrops for treasure hunts.

Archaeologists. Thanks to Indiana Jones and other movie adventurers, archaeology and adventure are somewhat synonymous these days. The game of Safari, which includes a search for an ancient tribal treasure, is just one example of how this theme can be used.

Extra Hints for Organizers

The story's the thing! All treasures have a story behind them and that story should be worked into the overall hunt. It can be a verbal story explaining something of the history of the area and of the treasure. Or it can be written down to include bits of information that will be important along the way. We have used both methods. When we prepare a written story, we have typically put it in the form of a ship's log or the "autobiographical" writings of the character who originally hid the treasure.

Finding the right treasure. We have already said that the treasure at the end of the hunt is not as important as the hunt itself, but using a treasure that fits the theme does make the hunt seem more authentic.

For a pirate hunt, make a couple of treasure chests out of medium-sized wooden boxes. These can be constructed out of scrap plywood and stained to look ancient and weathered. Paint a skull and crossbones on the lid and fill the treasure chest with costume jewelry, old boots, a giant trophy cup, and maybe even an old wedding dress (clothes are good space fillers).

You can invent many treasures for an Indian hunt. We have used a full headdress, some arrowheads, a giant stuffed bird (we called it The Great Winged Spirit), and several other items.

An archaeologist's treasure could be any number of things: old painted pots, ancient scrolls, tablets with hieroglyphics, golden idols (from the tops of old trophies), or royal Egyptian burial sites.

If the story involves a hunt for gold, cloth bags filled with rocks create a realistic treasure. Or even better spray paint porous rocks with gold before bagging them.

Not all treasure is buried treasure. We have put treasure in hollow trees, under rocks, in pipes, in chimneys, in caves, and have even suspended heavy treasure chests from the branches of a large oak so that they were out of reach for people on the ground.

Create small successes early. When we discussed treasure paths, we suggested leaving small helping items along the way. These items can be anything necessary to get to the big treasure. Included in this list might be shovels, keys, ropes, maps, and clues. If these are given early in the hunt, the seekers will feel they are on their way to the treasure!

Use variety in hiding places. If you are concealing small clues, try putting them in all kinds of hidden places. Put notes in the pockets of clothes, and lead the seekers to an old suitcase. Put a key in a bottle and leave it floating in a pool of water. Hide a clue in a letter and give out ten to be searched through. Bury a clue or two in the pages of a book on a fairly full shelf.

Have people work together. In some treasure hunts a few seekers do the work for the entire group. Try to include clues that will involve several people in the process. Measure the distance from one place to another by having ten people stand side by side. Use some math problems that will require the brainpower of players more advanced in math, or use literary references that demand knowledge of books that only a few people will have read.

Give names to natural objects. Who ever said a tree had to be called a tree? Why can't it be the mast of an old ship? And why can't telephone lines be telegraph lines? Changing the face value of natural objects is one of the best ways to make your hunt authentic. Small pools along a creek may become large bays. Tiny creeks may be passed off as raging, even famous rivers. Brick buildings might become old banks and large pipes can be called mine shafts. Let your imagination run wild. Once your seekers discover that all is not as it seems, their imagination will go more crazy than your own.

Use odd measurements. Instead of using steps or feet or degrees, try using some unusual form of measurement. How about the length of a shovel, bone, or stick? What if two people had to hold a string taut while standing on two secret spots, and the treasure is buried below a mark at an odd place on the string? These measuring devices can be placed at various stops throughout the hunt.

Secret spotting tools. Use a tool such as a pirate doubloon with a niche cut out of it. Have players find the location of a clue by standing in a precise spot, looking through the niche, and lining up the niche with some monument in the landscape.

Bring back old clues. At various places along the hunt's path, have seekers count objects. Tell them to remember these numbers. Later have them use these numbers (either alone or together in a mathematical equation) as the number of steps they should take, or the number of trees they should see, or any other numerical reference you might need.

CHAPTER ELEVEN

Bounty Run

BOUNTY RUN IS A TREASURE HUNT in which treasure seekers race to be the first to find the richest booty. Any combination of maps, riddles, and treasure paths are placed in a clue-to-clue pattern. The seekers find little treasures that have a point value and lead them to the next clue. The paths of the different teams of treasure hunters may often cross, and at those points hunters may steal from each other or trade needed items and information.

While Bounty Run is easy to run, setting up the game may take ten to twelve hours and more if you need to find or make the objects that will be hunted. The hunt itself will last four to five hours depending on the difficulty of the hunt and the players' abilities.

Teams and Players

Bounty Run may be played by groups of any size. It is best played by two teams, but can be played with any number of them. For the purposes of this chapter, we will assume that there are two teams. The players, called bounty hunters, may be of any age or size, but teams should be fairly balanced.

Each team has two special players who are called bounty runners. They should be given a special identifying mark. This identification can be a special shirt or hat, or an ink mark on the back of the hand.

The people involved in setting up the treasure hunt should participate in the game as sheriffs. If you set up the game alone, recruit at least one other person to be a sheriff also.

Stuff You Need

Ten-foot-square tarps. There should be one tarp for each team. Each team uses a tarp to hold their booty. Any item placed on a tarp cannot be stolen.

Pocket notebooks. Sheriffs each record the fines they levy during the game in their pocket notebooks.

Booty. These objects may be flags, notes, beads, cans, bottles, arrowheads, treasure chests, or almost anything. See the point chart on page 136 for more suggestions.

Master treasure map. As part of your setup before the hunt, you will need to draw a master treasure path chart and place clues or objects at each of the stops on the chart. Here is an example of a set-up chart for Bounty Run:

It is important to select names for each of the spots in the hunt, be they official names ("Fort Collins," "Treasure Island") or generic names ("fishing bridge," "swim-

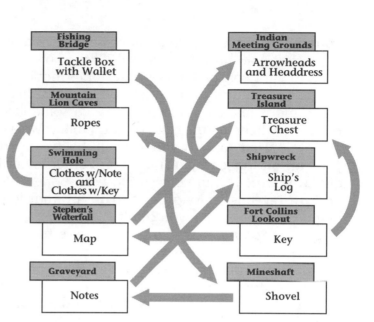

ming hole"). At each spot, know what clue you will give and where it will lead. Indicate where each clue will lead by arrows on your chart.

Maps and stories. These are the tools that the hunters need to find their clues and booty. Chapter Ten details how to create these materials.

Story and Rules

You may want to dress and talk Western, assume a tough role, and take the hunters outside.

"Good afternoon, folks. As you have undoubtedly been told, the area aroun' you is rich with treasure. Until las' weekend, Tracer Hill was a quiet place. Then them newspaper people had to do some searchin' aroun', an all you prospectors got to readin' that mebbe there's somethin' for ya up here. Well, maybe there is. I ain't the one ta say. But as long as yer in my jurisdiction, yer gonna abide by my rules. We cain't lose all law 'n' order 'round here just 'cause ya think ya got a right ta the place.

"Hold on a minute an' I'll turn over everythin' I know 'bout these parts to ya. I got some maps and stories that'll amaze ya. I'd just a soon give 'em to ya as have ya sneakin' 'round raisin' heck tryin' ta get ahold of 'em. These maps and stories should give ya some ideas 'bout where ta begin yer hunt. Now here are the rules ya gotta follow when ya start huntin'.

"*First rule*—if yore carryin' booty an' yore a reg'lar bounty hunter, you can git tagged by a hunter on t'other team. If you are tagged, ya gotta give whatever you are carryin' ta yore 'ponent. An ya cain't tag that person back in revenge so long as he's carryin' that loot. Any other hunter on yer team can tag him, but you cain't.

"*Second rule*—ya gotta choose two of yore hunters ta be bounty runners. They'll git a special mark so ya'll know who they are. Don't never tag a bounty runner and try an' steal what he's got without help. Ya can only steal what they got by surroundin' them with five people. These five people gotta make a circle, holdin' hands 'round a bounty runner. Once they got him surrounded, he has ta give the booty ta one o' the hunters. An' bounty runners, don't never steal from 'nother hunter.

"*Third rule*—each team o' you looters is gonna git a tarp. Ya can put this tarp on the groun' anywhere ya wish. When yore loot is on it, nobody can touch it. It can never be stolen legally. Still, ya should have a hunter stay near it just in case. Go 'head an' look at whut t'other team's got on their tarp, but don't ya dare snitch it! T'only way ta get somethin' off'n their tarp is ta trade fer it. Ya got that?

"*Fourth rule*—tradin' loot is okay by me. So long as the leaders of yer teams agree, any trade's fair. How ya make these trades is yore affair. Ya don't need ta clear yer trades with me or my deputies; we got enough trouble ta deal with.

"*Fifth rule*—ya cain't just go 'round actin' like ya own everythin'; not all the land 'round here is public land. Fact is, much of the area is private property. 'Cause all you treasure seekers come up here suddenlike, not all the owners had time to post no trespassin' signs. Still, if ya go on their property,

134

yore trespassin' and me or one of my deputies'll be forced ta fine ya. If'n we tag ya when yore on private land, we'll fine ya various amounts, 'pendin' on how much the owner hates people on his land or how many times we have already caught ya. We're gonna record all yer fines in our notebooks an' charge ya fer 'em at the end of this hunt.

"Use your haid when yore out huntin' treasure. If ya find somethin' just lyin' 'roun', it ain't booty. Treasure don't just lie around. But if you find somethin' with the help o' the clues, grab it. Ya'll prob'ly git some pretty good points fer it.

"That's all I got ta say. Good luck, and may ya find wonderful treasure!"

You should then answer any questions. The seekers need to understand that Bounty Run has no boundaries because the playing area is determined by the course of the hunt. Then hand out the tarps and any maps or stories you have to give the players and send them on their way.

The End and the Score

When you decide to end Bounty Run depends on how much time you have to play. It's best if you can play until all of the biggest treasures have been found. Sometimes the players do not get this far, however, so you may need to declare an end to the game. In this case, the teams still receive points for the booty that they have found. If you do have to end before the final treasures are found, you might want to leave those treasures "out there" for the players to find at a later time.

Scoring for Bounty Run depends on your hunt. For each item of booty or bit of information you hide, you need to determine a point value. The closer an object is to one of the big treasures, the more valuable it should be. Make sure to put together a predetermined list of the value of each object you hide. A typical Bounty Run point value chart may look like this:

Scoring Chart

Flags ....1,000 points
Notes ....2,000 points
Beads, cans, bottles ....3,000 points
Arrowheads ....4,000 points
Shovel, rope, bags ....4,000 points
Keys...5,000 points
Tackle box..5,000 points
Map...7,000 points
Treasure chest (unopened)..................5,000 points
Treasure chest (opened with key) ......25,000 points

You should gradually increase the point values of each item depending on the difficulty involved in finding them.

To score Bounty Run, first add together the values of all of the booty for each team. Then subtract any fines the sheriffs have levied during the course of the game (fines should range from 100 to 1000 points), and you have the final scores.

Rules and Advice for Sheriffs

As sheriff, you can control the game's length. If you need the game to go a little more slowly, show up often when hunters are getting close to important items. After all you know the hunt. The designation of public and private property is really up to you since none of the land is posted. Declare areas that have special booty private and chase the hunters away.

If you need to pick up the pace of the hunt, allow players to hunt unhampered in areas that contain important booty. You may also give hints to hunters. Tell them they are on private property, have them come talk to you and give them some information. Of course if you declare an area public land at one point, don't chase players off it later.

Extra Hints for Organizers

If Bounty Run still sounds overwhelming, refer back to Chapter Ten, Designing a Masterful Treasure Hunt. This chapter discusses in detail (complete with maps and charts) much of what we have discovered about designing effective treasure hunts.

Bounty Run: Outline of Rules

Scenario
Bounty hunters search for treasure on property that is loosely protected by local sheriffs.

Playing Time
Two to five hours or more.

Stuff You Need
one ten-foot-square tarp for each team
one pocket notebook for each sheriff
items needed for the treasure hunt (booty)
master treasure map

Characters
The organizers are the sheriffs who control the activities of the bounty hunters.
The players are the bounty hunters who search for hidden treasure. The players are split into two teams. Two players on each team are designated as bounty runners.

Object
1. The players use written stories or clues to begin hunting for treasure. From this information, they go to the possible places where they believe the hunt starts. Each new place offers a piece of booty and information leading to the

big treasures. Two or three big treasures are hidden at the end of the hunt.

2. The teams race to be the first to get to the big treasures. They accumulate information and gather as much booty as they can to earn points at the end of the hunt.

The Rules

1. If one player tags an opponent, the player may steal any object of booty or piece of information the opponent is carrying. When a player has booty stolen, that player may not seek revenge by tagging the player who stole it.

2. Each team has two players who are bounty runners. Five players must hold hands and surround the bounty runners to steal any objects that they are carrying. Otherwise, the bounty runners are free to carry objects without having them stolen.

3. Each team is given a ten-foot-square tarp. The teams place these wherever they wish. Any items placed on the tarps can never be stolen. As soon as one object has been placed on the tarp, the tarp cannot be moved for the rest of the hunt. (Although the objects on the tarp cannot be stolen, we recommend that one hunter stay and look after the booty.)

4. Teams may freely trade any objects or information they have with one another. These trades do not have to be cleared with the sheriff.

5. Any player tagged by a sheriff while on private property is subject to a fine. Because the property is not actually marked as public or private, it is up to the sheriffs to warn players that they are on private property. If the players are on private property, the sheriffs will try to chase them off the land. If the sheriff catches the offending player, the player will be subject to be fined from 100 to 1,000 points, depending on the location and nature of the offense.

Ending the Game

The game may end when the organizers wish or when all of the big treasures have been found. The head sheriff must make the decision when to end the game. When the game is over, all players return with their booty to the central meeting place. The scores are figured by adding the point values of the items of booty and then subtracting the amount of fines.

CHAPTER TWELVE

Adventure Games

Create Your Own
Adventure

Now that you understand how much fun great adventure games can be, you will no doubt want to create some of your own. If you have led some of these games, you have had to adapt the rules to fit your playing area, characteristics of the group, type of props available, and personal preferences.

When you make these small modifications, you are, whether you realize it or not, creating your own game. This chapter gives you the framework needed to take your creativity one step further; it gives you the tools necessary to organize your own ideas into adventure games unique to you and your group.

Creating an adventure game involves two steps: generating ideas and planning the game.

Generating Ideas

The first step in creating an adventure game is to generate as many ideas as possible. This is accomplished using a creative process called brainstorming. Brainstorming not only generates ideas but organizes and records those ideas on a list that can be used at a later time.

It is possible to brainstorm alone, but it is more productive when used in a group of two to five people. When we brainstormed the adventure games found in this book, one of us usually began the brainstorming session with an idea, often stemming from a theme or a prop. The person with the idea brainstormed alone initially and would come to the session with some preliminary thoughts and ideas. Then we brainstormed the game as a group, giving new but related ideas and adding to each other's thoughts. An electric excitement comes after a brainstorming session that motivates its participants to put the game into a playable form.

There are a few important guidelines to follow when conducting a brainstorming session. First, everyone in the group should feel the same freedom to contribute ideas. Second, no negative feedback should be allowed and no idea should be considered a bad idea. Often ideas thrown out in a brainstorming session sound wild and unworkable. But these ideas are often springboards to more workable ideas. Finally, every idea should be recorded for later reference. These notes are important so that none of the small details that can add to the game will be forgotten. It is helpful to designate someone not actively involved in the brainstorming session as note taker. Notes can be recorded on a flip chart or chalkboard so that the entire creative process is documented visually as it occurs. Or the session can be recorded on videotape or audiotape, if doing so will not stifle the spirit of the session.

How Brainstorming Begins

You can start creating your adventure game from a number of different angles, all of which are equally workable.

Game type. One way to start is to think about the type of game you'd like to create. Is your ultimate goal a chase game, a hunt game, a capture game, or a product of some combination? (Look back at Chapter Two if you need to review the types of games.)

Playing area. Another way to get started is to explore a field, park, campground, or other area that might make a good playing field for an adventure game. Walk slowly through it. Look high. Look low. Stoop to peer into the bushes or to climb a tree. Listen for sounds. Smell the air. Let your mind wander and imagine what story could take place there. Many of our hunt games were created in this way.

Equipment or props. Go to garage sales, junk yards, auctions, or any place where "stuff" accumulates. You will probably find hundreds of items that you could use in a game.

Story line. Use a story, time period in history, or theme to build a game. A personal or public library is a great place to start. Look through books, magazines, and newspaper articles. A local paper or historian can recount local legends and stories that can be used to make an adventure more exciting.

Existing games. You may want to take a game that your group already enjoys and add a story, props, and costumes to it. Build an adventure around the game. Outpost (Chapter Five) is a combination of tag and Capture the Flag onto which we imposed a battle story.

Planning the Game

Planning the game is the process of reviewing the ideas accumulated while brainstorming and then organizing them into a game plan. The game plan will consist of game elements (rules, teams, boundaries) and adventure elements (story, setting, props).

Game elements. There are seven elements to look at and each has several questions that need to be thought about and answered.

*Goal. What is the goal of the game? How do the players reach the goal? Is the game over when the goal is achieved? How many goals are there for each team? Does the team need to meet before it obtains the final goal? Is the goal too easy or too hard?

*Offenses and defenses. Are there any weapons? What are they (flags, hand tags, flashlights, flour-filled socks)? Who has them? How do they get them? What are their capabilities and guidelines for use? What obstacles stand in the way of the goal (a stream, a question to answer, clues, a number to guess)? How do players get back into the game (prison escapes, returning to the beginning)?

*People. Who are the individual characters in the story? What are their characteristics, capabilities, ranks? Are there teams? How is the group divided? How do the teams compete (against each other, against the leaders, or just for points)? What do the leaders wear? What do the players wear? Do they need to bring anything special to play?

*Boundaries. What are the outside boundaries? What are the boundaries of other areas within the playing area? Could people wander off (knowingly or unknowingly)? Are other activities including other people going on within or near the playing area?

*Scoring. Do you need a list of everyone playing and what teams they are on? What are the point values for all the goals? How are the point values going to be awarded? Do the actual point values need to be known by the players before the game? Can players cheat to get points unfairly? Are points going to be awarded for survival, clues figured out, escapes? Do you need a scoring chart? Is there a place to gather after the game for the players to tell their adventures and for you to announce the final scores?

Timing. When is the game to be played? If the game is to be played at night in the darkness, how bright is the moon going to be? Is there a meal break? How does the game fit into the group's schedule? How does what the group does before and after the game affect the game, and vice versa? Is there time to change clothes? When are things goint to be set up? Have you allowed time to give the rules and the final scores?

Communication. How will you announce or promote the game? When will you start promoting it? How will you give the rules, strategies, and assignments to leaders?

Adventure elements. There are still more questions you might consider if you are truly going to turn your game into an adventure. Let's see what these questions might be.

Characters. How many characters are there? What are their names? What is the narrator's character? What are the characters of any assistants, key leaders, and teams? What are their roles in the adventure?

Props and equipment. What do you need to enhance the story line? How can you make the props more authentic? What hats, makeup, and costumes can you get? What can you do to add sound to the adventure (e.g., music, sirens, noises)? What kind of food would add to the adventure?

Setting. How can you make the playing area match the theme of the game? How can you use lighting? What parts of the area, through imagination, can be used (e.g., a tree that can be a mast to a ship, a field that could be used as a graveyard)? Can there be a drama or an opening ceremony at the beginning?

Coherency. Are the players going after the appropriate goals for the story line? Does the story match the elements of the game? You don't have to be completely accurate, you just have to correct glaring errors that could take away from the adventure.

Wrapping it Up

When it is time for your players to relax at the end of a game, you still have some work to do. Make sure that you get some feedback from the players so that you can improve your game the next time that you play it. Ask the players and leaders how they liked the game. Ask how they think it could be improved.

And don't forget to write your game down so that others can use it. If you are interested in having it published, send us a copy. If we publish it, we will acknowledge you and send you fifty dollars. Send it to:

Hopper, Bernie, and Buck
c/o Youth Specialties Adventure Games
1224 Greenfield Drive
El Cajon, California 92021
How To Create Your Own Adventure

Outline

Brainstorming
You'll probably be most successful if you brainstorm with two or three others. Let your mind go on tangents, explore the seemingly silly. Don't throw out any idea. Don't be afraid of creating new, far-out ideas.

Different Approaches to Creating Your Game
You can use any of the following as your starting point for creating new games:

*Game type

*Playing area

*Equipment or props

*Story line

*Existing games

Wherever you start, the game needs to be made up of both game elements and adventure elements.

Planning the Game

1. **Goal.** Identify the goal of your game. How do you get to it? How do you return it to the start? Is it too easy? Is it too hard?

2. **Obstacles.** If the game is a chase or capture game, who has weapons? How are the weapons used? Are they leaders and/or members of the other team? What are the weapons? If the game is a treasure hunt, what kind of clues and obstacles do you want to have?

3. **People.** What will be the individual characters, ranks, characteristics, abilities of each of the players? How will the teams be divided? How will they compete? What will everyone need to wear and bring along? What will be each one's offense and defense?

4. **Boundaries.** What are the outside boundaries and the area boundaries? Is it safe to play at night? Can people get lost? Can people cheat?

5. **Scoring.** Do you need a list of everyone playing and which team they are on? What will be the point values for each of the characters captured? Are there bonuses for survival, extra points for certain clues?

6. **Timing.** Do you need to play at night or during the day? If you are playing at night, do you need to take into consideration the phase of the moon? Do you have other activities that you are planning the game around? Do you need to plan a meal break? Have you allowed time for rules (both leaders and players), preparation and set-up, story telling, and giving the final scores?

Planning the Adventure
Create the story and blend it into the game. Write it out. Make sure that you brainstorm the following:

1. **Characters.** What are the names and traits of the narrator, assistants, key leaders, players, teams?

2. **Props.** What kinds of props will add to the story? Consider costumes, music, food, and any other elements that will spice up your theme.

3. **Setting.** How will lights or night sprinklers and lights affect your game if you are planning to play at night? What suggestions can you make to your players so that the setting seems consistent with the game (will you need to make tree branches ship masts, for instance, or make streams roaring rivers)?

4. **Coherency.** Are the teams going after right goals? Does the story match the game and vice versa? You may want to have people not involved with the game listen to your plans to make sure that they are on target.

Communication

1. Do the leaders know the rules? Do they have all the props they need? Do they have everything they need to develop team strategy?

2. Have you rehearsed the story either in your mind or with another person? Do you need props or a specific setting to give the rules? What is the right timing for giving the rules?

Wells Fargo

WELLS FARGO is one of the most frequently played wide games. So many people have played the game in so many different ways that there just isn't a consensus about how it is to be played.

We provide two versions of Wells Fargo here. The first version is better suited for younger players, whereas the second version will probably be preferred by older groups. For game organizers experimenting with adventure games, Wells Fargo is a good place to begin. It's a simple game and does not require a large block of playing time.

Wells Fargo for Younger Groups

If you work with younger players, especially those of elementary or early junior high school age, you know that they often enjoy games that require lots of running and athletic involvement. This version of Wells Fargo will allow them to use their individual athletic abilities but also requires teamwork.

Teams and Players

Wells Fargo may be played by any number of people. The kids work as a group against the leaders. The kids are robbers who attempt to steal bags of gold, and the leaders are guards who must protect the gold until the stagecoach arrives. There should be one guard for every five or six robbers and at least three guards for any group larger than ten people.

Stuff You Need

Bags of gold. These should be cloth bags filled with a couple of pounds of sand or sawdust. The bags should be heavy enough to fly through the air but not so heavy that they would hurt a player who might miscatch one while running. There should be about three bags for every two guards. So if five guards are playing, you should have seven or eight bags of gold.

Playing Area

The playing area should cover at least one acre (about sixty-five yards by sixty-five yards) and have lots of hiding places—trees, rocks, and bushes. At one end of the playing area, is a "robbers' roost"—a safe zone for the robbers. It may be a ten-yard-wide strip (like a football end zone) or a thirty-foot circle. The robbers' roost does not need to be an especially large area.

Rules

Before the game the guards need to hide the bags of gold throughout the playing area. The bags must be hidden with at least some portion of each bag visible. If there are bags hidden in trees, they should be reachable from the ground. It's great if the guards can hide the bags while the robbers are busy with some other activity. This way the robbers aren't tempted to watch the guards hide the bags.

To begin the game, the robbers leave their roost and the guards spread out over the entire playing area. It is the job of the guards to protect the bags of gold, but they may not stand any closer than ten yards away from any bag of gold.

The robbers search the play area for the hidden bags. If a guard tags a robber who does not have a bag of gold, the robber must return to the roost. Once at the roost, the robber must count to fifty and then may return to play.

If the robbers find a bag of gold, they must try to get it back to their roost. They may run with the bag, hand it off to other robbers, or pass it through the air. If a robber carrying a bag is tagged by a guard, the robber must return to the roost and count to 100 before coming back into the game. The bag of gold is returned to its original hiding spot. Any bag falling to the ground while robbers are passing it is also returned to the spot where it was first hidden. (It usually takes the robbers several tries at each bag before they can safely get one to the roost. Encourage them to work as a team if they are having difficulty.)

Wells Fargo has no time limit. You may play for as long as you like, but it is best to play until the robbers are just winning. You can control the length of the game by periodically announcing how long it will be until the stagecoach arrives to pick up the bags of gold. It's easy to stretch the minutes this way, and the robbers should win the game by a bag or two.

The robbers win the game when they steal more bags than the guards have protected. The guards win if they protect more bags than the robbers have stolen.

Extra Hints for Organizers

If you want your players to feel more successful as they try to steal the bags of gold, you can make one small modification to the rules. When a guard tags a robber carrying a bag or when a bag falls to the ground, leave the bag where the robber is tagged or where it falls to the ground. If you play using this rule, also stipulate that the robbers cannot throw the bags forward (that is, in the direction of the robbers' roost).

Wells Fargo for Older Groups

The version of Wells Fargo that works best with older groups involves less running than the one for younger groups, but it is otherwise just as active. Pay special attention to the suggested precautions; this brand of Wells Fargo can get out of hand if players aren't careful.

Teams and Players

In the "older" version of Wells Fargo, the players are divided evenly into two teams, the Indians and the cowboys. The players do not need special costumes, and they may not wear hats.

One person needs to be stationed at the Indian village and another at the cowboy ranch. These people are not actively involved in the game, but must keep track of how many "scalps" they give out.

Stuff You Need

Bags of gold. These should be cloth bags filled with a couple pounds of sand or sawdust. There should be one bag for every two cowboys. If there are twenty cowboys playing, you should have ten bags.

Two rolls of masking tape. One roll of masking tape is needed for each team. Before the game, all of the players are given a short strip of tape to put on their foreheads. This piece of tape is the player's scalp. During the game the extra tape is kept at the Indian village and the cowboy ranch.

Playing Area

The playing area needs to be larger than the area in the first version. It should cover at least two acres (about 100 yards by 100 yards) and have lots of trees, rocks, and bushes where the bags of gold can be hidden. At one end of the playing area, establish a free zone known as the Indian village. This may be a ten-yard-wide strip (like a football end zone) or a thirty-foot circle. At the other end should be a similar area known as the cowboy ranch.

Rules

Before the game begins, the cowboys need to hide the bags of gold throughout the playing area. Each bag must be hidden so that some portion of it is visible. If a bag is hidden in a tree, players on the ground should be able to reach it. If possible have the cowboys hide the bags while the Indians are involved in another activity so the Indians will be less tempted to watch the cowboys hide the bags. The Indians must steal the bags of gold and return them to the village.

Before the game begins, all the players should put a short piece (about three inches) of masking tape on their foreheads. It is very important that the ends of the tape are free from the skin and not pressed down. These pieces of tape represent the players' scalps.

The Indians begin in the village and the cowboys begin in the ranch. When all players are ready, a signal starts the game. Players then spread throughout the playing area to steal or protect the bags of gold.

The Indians look for the hidden bags of gold first, while the cowboys attempt to protect the gold by scalping the Indians. The Indians then try to scalp the cowboys. A cowboy earns a scalp by removing the piece of tape from an Indian's forehead, and vice versa. Any player who is scalped must return to the village or the ranch to get a new piece of tape. Those people who are stationed at the village and the ranch must keep track of how many new scalps they give out.

When the Indians find a bag of gold, they try to steal it and get it back to the village, much as in the earlier version. They may run with a bag, hand it off to another Indian, or throw it through the air. If an Indian is scalped by a cowboy while carrying a bag of gold, the gold is taken to the cowboy ranch. If a bag falls to the ground while being passed or thrown between Indians, it becomes the possession of the cowboys and is taken to the cowboy ranch.

The game ends when all the bags have been taken either to the Indian village or the cowboy ranch. Unlike the first version of Wells Fargo, there is a scoring system for this game. Give the Indians 1,000 points for any bags they get to the village and 200 points for each cowboy scalp (as counted by the person in the ranch). Give the cowboys 1,000 points for any bags they get to the ranch and 200 points for each Indian scalp (as counted by the person in the village).

Extra Hints for Organizers

This version of Wells Fargo can be rougher than the first version. It's very important that the pieces of tape on the players' foreheads are not taped down on the ends. Tell the players to be careful when going for a scalp. To reduce the risk of someone's eye getting poked, you may want to have the tape put on the players' shoulders and have the girls put their hair in pony tails. Also, if you are playing with both boys and girls, you may want the girls to scalp the boys, but do not permit the boys to scalp the girls. Only girls should be allowed to scalp girls.